ABOUT THE AUTHOR

For 20 years Gavin Walker has worked as a marketing consultant for many companies helping them with their communications challenges. He has worked successfully with international organisations such as Hilton International, Avonmore Foods and Dessian although he specialises in working with small companies. Over the years Gavin has helped develop full marketing plans for small companies, giving them direction and raising their profiles in their local community.

He has recently been appointed editor of the Northern Business Mail in Belfast. However, he still works closely with his existing clients and is maintaining his consultancy business. Gavin lives in Groomsport, County Down, with his wife Margaret and three-year-old son Christopher.

Grab Their Attention!

Advertising and Promotion on a Shoestring Budget

Gavin Walker

Oak Tree Press

Dublin

Oak Tree Press
Merrion Building
Lower Merrion Street
Dublin 2, Ireland

© 1998 Gavin Walker

A catalogue record of this book is
available from the British Library.

ISBN 1 86076 086 4

Printed in the Republic of Ireland by Colour Books Ltd.

CONTENTS

PREFACE

There are two facts of life every one of us in business have to accept: (1) banks only lend money to people who already have it, and (2) the people who need the most help to promote their business have to do it themselves.

Unfortunately I can't do a lot to help you with the first reality, but I can help with the second.

Over the past 20 years I have worked for a number of international organisations, owned, operated and sold a few small businesses, and helped a lot of people with their challenges of communicating with their customers. Now as an award-winning copywriter I feel that I have the experience and knowledge to help others who, like me and thousands of small business men and women throughout the country, have to add "Promoter" to our list of daily different roles.

In a world that suffers from incredible over-communication, you have the responsibility of slicing through the noise and babble to get your message to your existing and potential customers. And because we live in this over-communicating world, you also have to choose the right media at the right price to get the best return on your advertising pound.

That's where this book will give you practical guidance and help. This is not an academic masterpiece full of graphs and jargon. Instead, it is a simple step-by-step guide which will show you how to get your business noticed by the people who matter: your existing and potential customers.

All over the country there are people like you and me who are reaching for a dream. People who have decided to go it alone in self-employment. They run their businesses from small shops, manufacturing plants, and even their back bedroom. Every one of us holds on to the belief that we can make our business something worthwhile that will grow strong and flourish and be a monument to our efforts.

We know that before us many of the big businesses of today started small and with effort and ability grew and grew. We've read all about the phenomenon of Apple Computers, Readers Digest and Xerox which each started as a dream in a garage. And we're determined to make our business something more than it is now.

To do that we know we have to spend time and money (although not necessarily a lot of money) in advertising and promoting our business. Because no matter how great our product or service, if nobody knows about it we're doomed to failure. The problem is: we're not too sure how to go about it effectively.

Well this book will answer most if not all of your questions about how to promote your business successfully and on a shoestring. It'll show you how to write ads that work and boost business. It'll show you how to put together a brochure that will sell product before it even arrives in your shop. It'll show you how to get new customers and how to get more money from your existing ones. And most importantly, it will show you how, with a bit of imagination and time, you will be able to promote your business absolutely free by presenting the media with stories they simply can't resist.

Your business can grow into something that is beyond your present imagination, but only if you are prepared to make it happen. Working with this book, you will be able to get your business noticed and enjoy steady growth year after year.

But don't wait until tomorrow to do it. There are people out there waiting, wanting to hear from you and you have a responsibility to get your message to them — today!

Good luck and keep reaching.

Gavin Walker
Groomsport, January 1998

I would like to dedicate this book to my wife Margaret who has given me the encouragement and support I needed to write it and my parents who have encouraged me to live the dream.

1

MARKET RESEARCH

Find out what they want — then give it to them!

Yes! Even your business needs effective market research

If you don't believe your business needs effective market research, then you've bought the wrong book! Think of it this way, if you don't know exactly what you customers want, then how are you going to sell them anything? How are you going to produce viable advertising? What are you going to say in your sales letter that will excite them?

In any case, there's nothing mystical, difficult or even costly about market research. In fact, I'm going to show you how to carry out effective market research that will make the difference between the success or failure of your business, and it won't even cost you a penny.

Mind you, if you do think your business doesn't need to do market research, you're certainly not alone. It's a constant source of amazement to me that so many of my clients — some of which are pretty big organisations — haven't the slightest idea if what they are providing is what their customers really want. Instead they're happy enough to bounce along on the seat of their pants betting on "intuition" to get them through.

So let me tell you now that unless you have researched the market demand for your product or service, and unless you've discovered your customers "hot buttons" — those all-important little things that will make them buy your service or product instead of the other fella's — then you are doomed to failure. Not immediately, maybe, but soon. And probably sooner than you think. The truth is, if you want your business to be one of the 20 per cent that will be still around after five years, you can't afford not to do market research.

Of course, the real problem with market research is the name. It conjures up visions of a small army of expensive experts travelling the length and breadth of the country accosting people in shopping malls and forcing them to answer hundreds of questions in minute detail.

And you could do that. You'd end up with a 200 page report with accompanying graphs and appendices. You'd have responses measured mathematically by the Hendry, Assessor, Sprinter or News models. And you would have a pretty good idea — although no absolute guarantee — of the viability of your product or service. You'd also have high blood-pressure and a bill that will give your bank manager apoplexy.

The good news is that while all of these methods are viable and valuable and carried out every day by the big players, you don't need them. But you do still need to get into the marketplace and find out what your competition is doing, how they're doing it and what they're charging for it. You also need to know what they're not doing. And you still need to find out what will make your potential customers buy your product or service instead.

And you'll need to do it every day if you want to stay ahead of the competition. Because if you don't do it, some other bright spark will and he'll start stealing your customers from under your nose by offering them something they want that you're not providing.

Why you should never assume people want what you're selling

Why, indeed. After all, isn't your widget exactly what the world has been waiting for? Haven't you spent countless hours and sleepless nights creating the perfect service that will simply sell itself? Well, here's some news for you: no you haven't!

Now I know just how difficult that might be to accept. But if you don't accept it right now, you'll never do the research necessary to find out the truth. And not knowing is going to be expensive. Either you'll spend a lot of money trying to convince people to buy something they don't want or you'll miss opportunities to maximise sales by missing those all important "hot buttons" that turn passers-by into customers.

Don't make the same mistake I come across so often. People get themselves so wrapped up in the minute details of their project that they lose sight of the big picture. They can tell you the cost of producing their service down to the last halfpenny. They can tell you the exact measurements of their widget. And they know precisely how many they need to sell to make their first pound. But what they can not tell you is either (1) who will buy this wonderful idea, or (2) what "hot buttons" they need to push to grab people's attention.

And frankly I don't care if you have the best mousetrap in the world. If people just don't want it, or if they don't know you've got it, then there's no way you're going to get into the starting box let alone reach the winning line.

That's why you must do market research. And that's why you must be prepared to accept the results of that research, even if it means throwing your ideas in the bin and starting all over again. The market is king for small businesses. You ignore it at your peril.

How to start doing worthwhile market research . . . right now!

There are two areas of research that every business ignores at its peril: (1) researching the competition and (2) researching what your customers want. Neither are difficult or require special training. Both require a bit of time and effort, and both are essential if your business is to be one of the 20 per cent that succeed.

1. How to find out what your competition is up to.

There's no mystery to researching your competition. If you're building a new widget, you send off for all the brochures on widgets available in your area. You study the brochures carefully, call the sales office and get a look at as many of them as possible to see where their strengths and weaknesses are.

Likewise, if you're offering a new service you go and see all the existing service providers and ask them lots of questions about what they offer. What do they charge? When are they available? How easily available are they? How quickly can they react to a call? Anything that will give you a profile of their business and pinpoint what they are not offering, or where you could offer something better and/or cheaper.

And if you're already in business you have an even greater need to do research on your competitors — every day if possible.

A client of mine, Jim, owns a barber shop in a small town. Every day he walks around the town and visits the other barber shops and salons. Over the years he has built up a rapport with all of his competitors and they have all become friendly rivals. So when any of them introduces a new idea, a new pricing structure or the slightest change in their operation Jim knows about it immediately and calls me to discuss how he should react to it. Sometimes there's no need to react at all. Other times we have a response in place and advertised even before the other shop has theirs in their window!

Now that's what researching your competition and keeping on top of what's happening in the marketplace is all about. There's no mystery to it, but the businessperson who doesn't do it is liable to end up with more time on their hands than they had bargained for sitting around wondering where their customers have gone.

2. How to find out what your customer wants.

The primary purpose of your market research is to find out about what your customers want and then giving it to them. And how do you do it? Well . . . you ask them.

Let me say that again because this is the most important piece of technical advice I have to offer. If you don't use any other tips or ideas in this book, use this one:

Ask your customers what they want — and then give it to them!

It sounds simple. It is simple! So why doesn't every businessperson do it every day with every customer? Let me ask you this, when was the last time a small business person asked you what you thought of their product or service? When did they say to you, "Thanks for your business. How could we serve you better?" or, "Tell me, did you have any difficulty finding this widget on the shelves? If we put them over here would they be easier to find?"

It just doesn't happen. But it should. A lot of the bigger companies do it as a matter of course, and they keep getting bigger. Try buying a new car and you'll see what I mean. Just when you've had time enough to figure out what all the knobs and buttons are for, you'll get the phone call.

> "So, Mr Walker what do you think of your new car? What about the seats, are they comfortable? And is there enough head room? What about the boot. Is there enough space there and should we put more light in there? And how's the . . . "

And so it goes on until they note every good and bad point about the car. All your answers go into the computer and the manufacturer soon knows what to add or take away to make next year's model even more appealing. To make it better . . . to sell more . . . to make more money . . . to get bigger . . . to stay ahead of the competition.

So please, please start doing the same thing for your business today. It doesn't matter whether yours is a seed of an idea, or has been around for three generations, you've got to start asking your existing and/or potential customers what they think about your business. And you've got to encourage them to be honest with you.

People love being asked their opinion and I can assure you they will be honest if you ask them to be. It mightn't happen the first time because they'll be too busy getting over the shock of actually being asked their opinion! But the next time you ask you can be sure they will be ready with ideas. Then they'll actually start to get involved with your business. Then they'll find themselves caring about your business. And then they'll give you ideas you could never have thought of because you're too close to the coal face. Even if you were your own customer you still wouldn't be able to see things "real" customers can see and experience.

So start asking questions today — and keep asking them.

How to ask questions that get the answers you need

It's quite possible for you to talk to somebody all day and walk away knowing lots about them as people, but nothing that will help you develop your business. So the first thing you must do is decide exactly what you want to learn from your research. You might want to know people's reaction to a particular idea you have. Or you might want to discover how people feel about a change in your pricing structure. Or you might even want to discover a whole list of things that will help you decide whether or not to proceed with a project.

No matter what or how much information you're looking for, you must be clear of what it is. Then you'll be able to develop specific questions and lead conversations to conclusions that give you the answers you need. And no matter how much or what information you're looking for, the method of asking questions remains the same.

You need to master the differences between "open-ended questions" and "closed-ended questions". They both have their place in market research, so we need to have a look at how they work and where to use them.

Open-ended questions are used to get your customers or potential customers talking. They encourage them to give you more than one word answers by starting with words like:

- How ("how do you think people might get to my shop?")

- Where ("where would you suggest I advertise my service?")

- What ("what do you think of this for an idea?")

- When ("when would you use this product the most?").

Asked in this way, people are almost forced into sharing their thoughts with you.

Once you've got them talking, it's important to be sure of what they are saying. You must not allow yourself to walk away from any research *thinking* you knew what they meant. Be absolutely positive. It might make the difference between success or failure. And to achieve this you start to use closed-ended questions, ones which only allow for one word or specific answers. Closed-ended questions are ones like "is this exactly want you mean?" or "do you think this is the best colour?"

Think about the way you ask your questions and be sure to vary your use of open and closed-ended questions as you go along depending on the responses you get from your customers.

Here's an example of both techniques in a short conversation:

> "Excuse me, could you tell me where you think I should advertise my business?" (Open question looking for customers ideas.)
>
> "Well. The local paper would be a good starting point. And then there's always the window at the supermarket, you could put a few ads up there."
>
> "Good idea. Is that the supermarket at the top of high street?" (Closed question here the only answer could be yes or no. Getting an absolute understanding.)
>
> "Yes."

And if you really want to hear an expert using these techniques you need go no further than your local office equipment dealer. Those guys are trained to be masters of using of using open and closed-ended questions to find out exactly what you're looking for — and then selling it to you!

How to encourage your customers to talk to you — every day

Part of the challenge of owning a business is that you wear 20 hats in the course of your day. One minute you're the salesman, then the bookkeeper and then the janitor. Every day is more exciting than the last.

But sometimes you can be taking on so many new things that others get put aside or join the "I'll do that tomorrow" pile, which is often where market research ends up. And as we all know, tomorrow never actually arrives.

So, if you're serious about doing your market research every day, then you need to put systems in place that will automatically trigger a response from your customers and keep that research engine grinding on. Nothing will replace you taking time out of your day to ask customers their thoughts. But having a system in place will at least mean you won't have to beat yourself up on the days when you really didn't have time.

Your system will be unique to your business, but here are two "musts":

1. **Create a response card.** One that allows your customers to share their thoughts and feelings with you. If you have a premises of some sort, get a "Customer Response Card" in place and put it somewhere where customers can see it and use it. In fact, train your staff to give them out to every customer they talk to. These cards can be as specific or general as you like, but I would recommend easy-to-answer questions like "is our service to the standard you expect?", along with a couple of lines for them to expand their answer if they desire. If yours is a

service business where you seldom see your customers, then get your response card off with every invoice you send, or create a thank you letter with response card to acknowledge payments.

2. **Get your staff involved.** Depending on the type of your business, you might find that your staff are more in touch with your customers on a daily basis than you are. If so, train them to ask the questions and write down their findings. Open a comments book for them to jot down notes of customer comments or thoughts. You should also encourage them to make a note of any ideas they have themselves.

Most importantly, read and react to the response cards and the comments book. They're a waste of time unless you do. It wouldn't be the first time a valuable customer would have been lost if the business owner hadn't reacted quickly to a negative comment on a response card.

Plus, with some tweaking and thought, your system can save you from making serious and expensive errors. Here's a great example of how a research system helped one of my clients make the right customer-oriented decision which in turn directly affected her profitability.

Paula owns a 15-room hotel with a small bar and a 50-seater restaurant in a very pretty village about 30 miles from a major city. People travel to the hotel in droves at the weekends because of its well-deserved reputation for great food. During the week local people provide a brisk lunch trade. But Paula's problem was dinner time mid-week. It just wasn't happening. And because she had to keep her staff on all week, it was beginning to really kill the profit.

When we met she had decided to place a number of ads in local papers within a 30 mile radius advertising a 20 per cent reduction on her dinner menu Monday to Thursday. My job was to create the ads. Not a tough job and I could have done everything quickly and left. But something didn't seem quite right.

"Who is your target market here?", I asked her. Well, she wasn't terribly sure, but thought it would be the same sort of people that visited on weekends. Fairly well-off couples who could afford to spend a few bob on dinner during the week and the discount would be enough to entice them to drive the extra few miles to her hotel — she hoped.

"And have you asked them if they are prepared to do that?" I asked. Her blank look said no.

The time had come for a little market research. And after some further discussion we decided to use the opportunity to put both a system for market research into place and to widen the scope of questions to get as much information as possible. We devised a simple and inexpensive "three-pronged attack" to find out what her customers actually wanted:

1. We created a table tent card asking for customers' thoughts on their experience in the restaurant and if they would be prepared to come for dinner during the week to take advantage of a discounted price.

2. We trained the head waiter to ask every guest how they had enjoyed their experience. Not the usual quick pass by asking the question when everybody's

mouth was full of food. But when the coffee was being served and the guests would be relaxed enough to answer questions honestly.

3. We created a book in which all of the waiting staff were asked to note guest comments — good and bad — as they heard them either directly or indirectly. They were also encouraged to add their own thoughts and ideas.

Result: within two weeks we had enough information to realise that far from advertising cheap dinners to people 30 miles away, there was actually a latent demand from the local townspeople for a set-price, all-inclusive high tea during the week. We created the advertising, placed it in one local paper and throughout the hotel, and watched mid-week evening sales triple almost overnight.

By making the system a permanent feature of the dining room — and in fact extending it to the bedroom business — we have been able to react to problems and demands quickly, effectively and profitably.

How to listen actively

But all of this would have been for nothing if Paula had not been prepared to react to the results of the research. Setting up a high tea menu involved quite a bit of work. Kitchen staff needed to be rescheduled. Pricing had to be reworked to offer good value at a profit. Administrative systems had to be put in place. And for the initial research table tents were printed and valuable time was spent training the staff to listen for and record customer comments.

How much easier it would have been just to forget the whole thing and advertise the 20 per cent reduction on dinner prices midweek. And how much less profitable!

Research works, but only if you are prepared to hear what people are actually saying — only if you are prepared to "actively listen".

A friend of mine has recently started training as a counsellor for a voluntary organisation. It's pretty in-depth training, but real emphasis is placed on learning how to become an "active listener". And those of us in business would do well to take the same course.

However, assuming we don't have the time, here's how a recognised expert in counselling, Gerard Egan, describes active listening: "the goal of listening is the kind of understanding that can serve the client's concerns." In other words, you have to listen with a completely open mind to what your customer is telling you and where possible be prepared to make what they are asking for available to them.

So when you ask your customers what they think, you must be prepared to hear what they are saying without the filters that we usually have in place. You must take every word they say, along with the tone in which they say it, and analyse it from their point of view, not your own.

For example, if somebody says, "I like your idea, but I don't think you'll be able to sell them at that price," don't just hear the first bit. Hear it all, analyse it completely, and then use your judgement and research to decide if they are right.

Everybody's point of view on your business is valid. Do not write somebody off as a dunce just because they haven't told you your idea, product or service is the best thing since sliced bread!

After 30 years in the civil service, Harry took advantage of an early retirement package, moved away from the city and he and his wife bought a corner shop in a small country town.

This was a dream come true for Harry. He had always wanted the freedom of self-employment and loved the idea of building up a nice business that he and his wife could run together. He was also looking forward to enjoying the great fishing in a local river.

And, of course, the shop was perfect. The last owner had let it run down a little, but it was on a fairly busy road at the entrance to an estate of houses, and beside a bus stop into the market town 15 miles away. This was going to be great!

The only thing Harry wasn't too sure about was what hours he should open. So he decided to do a little market research and go and ask his potential customers exactly what they wanted. So far, so good.

But just as he walked out the door his wife said, "I really wouldn't want to be open past 7:00 p.m., Harry. After all, we do need a bit of time to ourselves."

And with that ringing in his ears, he started knocking doors and asking his one question. The first few said he would need to stay open until 10:00 p.m. to catch many of the residents as they headed off to the night shift in the nearby factory. And then no less than three retired people in a row said they thought 7:00 p.m. was late enough. "After all," they said, "it's just not safe on the streets after dark, is it? I certainly don't know anybody who would dream of going out after 7:00 p.m."

And so 7:00 p.m. it was. His research showed that was the perfect closing time. Harry was happy and his wife was happy. Unfortunately, most of their customers weren't happy and decided that if Harry wasn't prepared to stay open when they needed him, they weren't going to use his shop. Instead, they passed him by and walked the extra quarter mile to the other shop in town who was always open when they needed it.

After six months, Harry contacted me in absolute desperation. His life savings were disappearing before his eyes and his previously happy marriage was dissolving under the pressure.

In fact, when we met, I thought he was going to cry. We talked and decided to have another go at research. This time, I went with him and we rediscovered what he had been told the first time round: 10:00 p.m. was the time to close. We also discovered that a lot of the people going on night shift would be prepared to pay for a packed "lunch", a service which Harry and his wife immediately made available and which we advertised in a door-to-door leaflet drop.

After a lot of hard work building customer confidence Harry is seeing his business turn around. Now nobody, but nobody, leaves his shop without having answered some question about how he could serve them better. He listens to every one of them — and acts on what they suggest.

What you can expect to achieve from market research

So now you've decided to do your research. You've put everything in place, your questions written and your pencil sharpened. So what can you realistically hope to achieve from your market research? Well, actually, anything you want. But specifically you can:

• Find out and react to what your customers think of your business.

• Find out and react to how your customers rate your business in comparison to your competitors.

• Find out how your new idea, service, product would be accepted and if it really is a "winner".

• Find out and react to your customers' "hot buttons" — what colours, lighting, services, pricing structure, etc. will make them choose to do business with you instead of the other guy in town. How should you advertise your service or product to get the best return from your investment.

• Find out exactly who your customers are — your "target market". What sex, age and income level they have. Where they live. Where they work. What papers they read. What radio station they listen to.

• Find out and react to your customers' changing demands.

• Find out if you need to review your pricing or add extra value.

• Find out if your customers would be prepared to pay more for higher quality.

- Find out if your ads or other promotions are working.

All of this information — and probably lots more that you can think of relevant to your specific business — can be discovered by going out and asking your customers and potential customers what they think.

And most importantly, it won't cost you a penny to get all of this information. Information which will make the difference between success and failure. Information which is absolutely invaluable to your business. Information which will make the advice and help provided in the rest of this book actually mean something as you create ads that work, direct mail pieces that get results and press coverage that boost sales.

Get the info, hit their "hot buttons" and grab their attention.

A case study: Alan starts a business from home

The business that needs most work put into market research is the one that doesn't exist — yet. There are no customers to bounce ideas off, and there's no shop or office to put customer response cards into. All you've got is an idea and a belief that this one is a winner. So how do you find out if you're right?

Alan found himself in just such a position. One evening he and a friend had been chatting. His friend was a freelance graphic designer who worked from a small one-man studio and was saying how disruptive it was to have to answer the telephone when he was in the middle of a project. His dilemma was that most people refuse to leave messages on answering machines and as he didn't want to miss important calls he always had to answer the phone. When his friend left, Alan started to think about a potential business idea. He would offer people like his friend an answering service with a difference. Using up-to-date telecom services, he would let them redirect their calls to his phone when they wanted either the peace to finish a project or were away from their office. He would install the equipment to tell where the call was being redirected from so he could answer the telephone in the name of that company. Clients would call for messages when it suited them best.

When he called me to ask my opinion I thought it was brilliant. Here was a simple idea that could be started fairly inexpensively and worked from home. But would there be a demand? It was time to do some market research. We decided we needed to know the following:

1. Was there a demand for this service? Our initial thoughts were that it would appeal to freelancers of all types and one-man offices including engineers, accountants, solicitors and consultants.

2. If they wanted the service, would they expect it to be available 24 hours-a-day, 7 days-a-week, or just during office hours?

3. Would they be interested in this simple answering service, or would they prefer a full secretarial-type service including fax bureau?

4. If they wanted the full service, would they like a one-off monthly charge, or would they prefer to be

billed a basic fee for the answering service and a per-use fee for the rest?

There were a lot of other areas we wanted to cover as well, but if we could get the answers to these questions, we would know if there was the demand for the answering-service and/or the secretarial service, and what people were prepared to pay.

First stop was Alan's freelancing friend to ask him his thoughts. Yes, he liked the idea, but would only be interested in the answering service. He would be prepared to pay around £20/25 per month for the service and would only need it during office hours.

Next stop was the local Yellow Pages to make a full list of possible groups of customers. We also went through the local Chamber of Commerce membership.

Now we had questions and a list of what we thought might be our "target market". We decided the best approach would be a short letter to introduce the idea, and a follow-up call three days later to determine interest.

We chose three companies from each of the classifications and got the names of the principles by calling and asking. We composed the letter and said Alan would be calling to follow-up to ask their opinion of the service and how it might be improved to help them. We mailed 100 letters.

Three days later — time enough for the letters to be received and read and soon enough to still be remembered — Alan called every one on the list and asked them his four questions. He made notes on their responses. At the conclusion of the conversation he asked them if they would like to subscribe to the service.

At the end of the marathon phone session he had talked directly to 79 people and had left 21 messages on answer machines.

He had discovered:

1. Accountants, solicitors and engineers had no interest in this service.

2. Freelance creative people — graphic artists, photographers, writers — liked the idea of being able to complete projects without the interruption of the telephone.

3. Small businesses/one-man-bands thought the answering service was excellent and might use the secretarial service.

4. Fifteen people had agreed to take the service for a trial period of three months at £25 per month or £69 if they paid the full amount up-front.

Then we analysed all the information we had and:

1. Decided that the response was positive enough to start.

2. Decided not to offer the secretarial service at all as there was little demand for it.

3. Created a sales letter specific to people in the "creative" categories offering the specific benefit of their being able to complete projects uninterrupted.

4. Created a sales letter to small businesses plugging the specific benefit of never having to miss a call again.

5. Decided to offer the same pricing structure to everybody, i.e. £25 per month or £69 for three months if paid up-front.

6. Realised that this service could be made available to any business throughout the country and created a "Six Month Development Plan" to take the business nation-wide.

Within the 6 months Alan had developed a client base of 70 customers netting him £19,320 per annum, and his list is still growing. His initial market research had told him he had an idea which would work with a specific target market at a certain price structure. Now he includes a short questionnaire with his monthly invoices asking his customers' views on a particular aspect of his service or possible new service. And every month he gets back a 70 per cent response which gives him enough information to know what will or will not work.

Ten Points to Remember

1. Very few businesses are unique. Either somebody else is already doing it or will soon start. Therefore:

2. No business can survive without market research.

3. Market research must be done on customers and competitors.

4. No advertising can be effective unless it appeals to your customers' "hot buttons" which you identify through research.

5. Market research does not have to be expensive.

6. Nobody will buy a product they don't want or don't know about.

7. Market research is simply about asking questions that invite honest answers.

8. Successful research is ongoing. You must develop a system which encourages you to ask questions every day.

9. You must learn to listen actively. Get rid of the filters and take notice of every comment made by every existing or potential customer about your business.

10. Start doing your market research right now.

2

DECIDING ON AN ADVERTISING STRATEGY

How to get the most from your advertising

What is advertising and do you need it?

As soon as you decide to create a letterhead, have a business card printed or employ a sign-writer to put your name over your shop, you've started to advertise. From then on everything you do that makes even one more person aware of the existence of your business is advertising.

But what is advertising? Why do we spend so much money on it? And, do you really need it?

Well, first, here's what it's not: advertising is not entertainment and it is certainly not art. That's not to say that your advertising shouldn't be entertaining or creative, but your sole goal is to make your cash register ring louder and more often. It is not to make people laugh or be amazed by your creativity. If you can be comical or creative and still get your message across clearly, then by all means do so. But it's not easy to do both, and I would be very cautious about trying. So here is a definition for your advertising:

> Your advert should be created in such a way as
> to inform your target market of your ability to
> meet their needs or wants and to create in that
> target market a desire to use your product or
> service in preference to any others available in
> the marketplace.

I think that is the longest sentence I have ever written!
However, if your ad meets these criteria, you won't go
wrong.

So, if that is what advertising is, do you need it? And
if you need it, how much of it do you need?

Whether you've already started in business or are
considering doing so you will have two recurring
dreams. One is that your business becomes successful,
grows and expands world-wide. The other is that no
matter what you try nobody has the slightest interest in
doing business with you and you fail miserably. However, as you've already done the market research that
assures you there is a need for your product or service,
your chances of success are greatly enhanced if you are
able to get your message to your potential customers.

That's where advertising plays its part for every single business from window-cleaner to multinational
company. The difference is in the scope and approach
of that advertising. One might decide that a simple
leaflet drop through 500 doors in a particular neigh-
bourhood will be the extent of the advertising while the
other takes 30 second spots on prime-time television
three times a day seven days a week in 10 countries
around the world. The approach is very different, but
the desired result is exactly the same: build the aware-
ness within the marketplace, develop a customer base

and then keep it. Advertising is the link between your business and your customers. Think of it as your "sales force" going out to sell your products. It must get to the right people and say the right things at the right time if it is to be successful. Before you even begin to consider creating your advertising you must decide who your target market are, where they are and which advertising medium gives you the best opportunity to reach them.

How to set your advertising priorities

Let's face it, your first advertising priority is simple: get as many customers buying your product or service as often as possible with the highest possible profit margin. Wrap it up in as many nice words as you like, that's the bottom line. But to make that happen you need to be aware of a lot of different factors that will affect the success of your advertising. So before you actually prioritise your advertising, look at how your customers decide where, when and what to buy by reviewing the "Customer Buying Cycle".

This cycle determines that before any of us even venture from our homes to buy a product or service we have already begun a very careful if sometimes subconscious selection process. We have, in fact, begun selecting our purchase by reviewing the available advertising of that product or service. We've had a look through the newspapers and magazines we subscribe to. We've digested the direct mail pieces that have dropped on the doormat. We've opened the commercial pages of the telephone book to see who provides the product/service locally and we might even have had a look at what's being said on the Internet. Having made this initial selection we then wander off to the shops or offices whose names have cropped up in our selection process. Only after making contact with that business will we actually decide whether or not we want to buy from them. Advertising has got us there in the first place and here's how it has all worked as determined by the US Small Business Administration:

1. We become aware of a product or service through advertising.

2. We decide whether or not to find out more about it based on the advert's appeal.

3. We go into the marketplace to investigate further.

4. We analyse what's on offer and compare value.

5. We make our final decision at the point of sale (and remember that might even be by simply deciding whether or not we trust the voice of the salesperson on the other end of a telephone).

From this buying cycle it is obvious that the reason for advertising is to spur your target market to make contact with you and give you the opportunity to make the sale. Therefore you must prioritise what, where, when and how you advertise as follows:

1. What aspects of your business will you advertise?
Your market research will hopefully have given you the answers to this question. Do your customers want you

to provide a better or faster service than your competitors? Do they prefer price cuts, or good value? Do they care about the cost at all? Do they use your shop because your staff are well trained and courteous? Will they use your service because you have developed a good personal reputation in another business before starting out on your own?

Whichever aspects of your business your market research have shown to be the most positive or in demand those must be the ones you concentrate on in your advertising.

2. *Where will you advertise?*

Different advertising media offer different advantages as discussed in detail later in this chapter. But an important part of your prioritising is to decide which available medium will achieve your goal. Advertising is always expensive if you don't get the return you wanted on your investment. But it's dirt cheap when it far exceeds your expectations. Therefore, where you choose to place your ads needs to be given a lot of careful thought. Believe me, when ad salesmen get a whiff of your budget you'll get calls from every newspaper, billboard company and printer that ever thought of doing business in your area. So be one step ahead by knowing that your choices are the right ones for you based on your own research. Be confident in your decisions and don't change them every time a new advertising person tries to sell you ad space.

3. When should you advertise?

Timing your advertising campaigns to get the best from them is extremely important. You will know your business and community better that me, but as a rule of thumb keep your advertising campaign going all year with particular emphasis on when you are already busy.

Yes, the best time to invest the most money on advertising is when you're busy, not when you're slow. A lot of small businesses make the mistake of trying to create business during their slack times by spending heavily on advertising. If they're very lucky it might bring in a little more business. But more often than not they'll find they're bucking the market and wasting their money. The only time it is wise to advertise during an apparent slack time is if you know decisions are being made at that time for future business.

Mary and Ned had always wanted to own a small restaurant. Mary was a good cook and Ned was a good accountant and they thought they could make a go of it. They were both outgoing and popular in their area so when a small bistro came up for sale they had a good look at the market, did their sums and bought it. From day one it was a great success and they soon developed a good regular clientele.

The first Christmas Ned decided he would like to really boost business by advertising in the local paper for office parties. Three adverts and £450 later he had only had five calls and one booking for four, and he pulled the ad. So this was the one thing he wanted to chat about in our first meeting early in the new year.

He just couldn't understand why other restaurants had a great Christmas party season and they hadn't. The answer was simple: timing. They had followed the rule of advertising heavily at the "money-spending time", but they had missed the boat by not advertising at the "decision-making time". Office parties are booked in early autumn and restaurants in their area had advertised at that time and sewn up the business before Ned and Mary got themselves organised. The following autumn they too advertised in September and October and had a very successful Christmas period.

You need to know when your customers are making their buying decisions as well as their actual purchasing to determine when to advertise.

In general, however, if your business has a slack time it's probably because your customers aren't interested in what you have to sell at that particular time. So spend a higher percentage of your budget to advertise your business at the times when it will increase sales. Spend highest at times when your customers are already thinking about spending money on your product/service. Do not try and buck the market. It won't work, and it'll cost you a lot of wasted money you can't afford trying to do it.

4. How will you advertise?

Your advertising "goals" will probably change according to where your business is on the "growth cycle" and on certain seasonal demands.

For example, if your business is just starting up your goal will be to get that fact to your target market as quickly, efficiently and cost-effectively as possible. If, on the other hand, you've been around for a while your goal might be to develop a theme of "unsurpassed choice", "guaranteed value for money" or "the best service in town".

At other times your "goal" might be to move stock by offering a cut-price throughout your shop or promote a particular range of goods or services that are pertinent to a certain season or event. The "goal" of your advertising will therefore determine how you advertise.

How to spend your advertising budget most effectively

It seems like every time you turn around somebody is trying to sell you advertising space in what will be the "best ad opportunity this year". They'll show you facts and figures that will convince you that if you don't sink every penny of your advertising budget into this one vehicle then your business is doomed. And if you say no they'll suddenly remember that they are offering a 35 per cent discount to new customers! Believe me, it happens. As soon as you raise your head above the parapet and say "I'm in business and I'm spending money on advertising" you'll be the most popular person in town and your phone will ring off the hook.

So the only way to avoid spending your money on advertising that won't give you a good return on your investment is to decide beforehand exactly what will, set out your budget and then stick to it. It won't be easy, but you've got to look at every advertising possibility with the jaundiced eye of "what's in it for me", not "how can I help put this advertising salesman's first born child through university!"

Be aware of what the statistics say about where your market is. You know more about your business and community than anybody (at least you should!), but if your business is a retail premises then you should know that:

- Independent shops will draw more than 80 per cent of their customers from within a half mile radius

- Chain stores probably get most of theirs from within a mile

- If your shop is in a shopping centre then your customers might come from as far away as 5 miles.

These figures apply only to shop owners, obviously service providers will usually do business in a larger area and mail order operators can consider the world their marketplace!

With all of this information in the back of your mind you are now ready to consider where to spend your hard earned and precious advertising budget. Every pound spent must show a substantial return, so think carefully about where to spend. When an ad salesman is talking to you about what they can do for you always hear them out, and then think it out.

1. Newspaper advertising

The vast majority of all advertising spending by small businesses is in newspaper advertising. And for good reason. Newspapers are popular amongst a wide cross-section of the population and either daily or weekly papers are often the first stop for people looking for suppliers of particular goods or services in their area. Even better news is that each newspaper sold has 3 readers on average. So you can safely multiply the sales of your local paper by 3 to find out the number of people who will at least see your ad.

One thing you have to remember about newspaper advertising, however, is that only placing an ad once won't work. In fact, you would be better not doing it rather than wasting your money. (The same applies to all advertising.)

You have to be prepared to repeat your ad over and over regularly. Because far from breeding contempt, familiarity with your ad will build recognition and trust. It shows you're serious about what you're doing and you're going to be around for the long haul.

Consumers are naturally conservative and take a while to get to know your business and what you have to offer. You know you have the best business in town, but many of your customers are going to take a while to decide that for themselves. Give them, your business and your choice of paper the opportunity to get to know each other and don't give up just because your one ad didn't have the phones ringing off the hook or lines of customers outside your door. Decide you're going to give an ad or a paper a certain length of time to succeed or fail before you decide to keep or dump it. I would suggest sticking with a paper for 2-3 months advertising at least once a week if you want to get a feel for how effective it's being.

Once you've got what you really believe to be the right message in a clear and attractive ad, don't be tempted to mess about with it. Let it sit with your potential customers and give them the opportunity to respond to it.

Newspapers are also usually fairly good value for money, allowing you to advertise regularly without breaking the bank. So, for many small businesses — especially retailers — advertising in your local paper might be the only advertising you need to do.

But which is your "local paper"? Take a look at your area and see just how many papers are available. There'll be the national papers, the regional papers, the local papers, the free newsheets, the specialist papers and probably even some you've never heard of that are being supplied solely to parents of your local school or members of local churches.

So, when you actually research the newspaper market you'll find that even here there are countless ways for you to spend your money. Which means you have to look carefully at the areas they cover, their circulation numbers and their rates.

National papers. The majority of small businesses will find that the national papers are irrelevant to their needs. But do take time to find out about any plans they might have for featuring your area. You might well find their rates for such a feature would be comparable to your regional papers and might even be worth the investment as a one-off if you are offering a product that would appeal to a wider audience than your local community and feel that your budget will stretch to a little experimentation.

Regional papers. Regional newspapers need to be approached in the same way. Sure they might have a great circulation of many thousands of copies, but if a lot of that circulation is in areas where there is little or no chance of the people travelling to buy from you, then give it a miss.

Local papers. The most ideal paper is the one which covers your exact catchment area of a mile or so. This might mean advertising in a free newspaper that is delivered door to door, or getting a space on a coupon drop that is done only every two or three months. But if these papers are being circulated to the doors of your target market then it doesn't matter that the circulation numbers are relatively small or that the papers don't have any great amount of prestige. The only thing that is important to you and the success of your business is that your potential customers read your ad. So find and advertise in the papers that get read by the people you want as customers.

Mark came to me to discuss setting himself up as a painter and decorator in a town of around 40,000. He had five years experience with a small company and really felt this was something he wanted to do. But, as is the case for all of us, his main concern was how to find a steady stream of customers.

We discussed a number of options, including writing a letter to all of the people he had done work for over the five years on the thinking that their homes might be ready for a "touch-up" again. We designed a number of fliers for door-to-door drops in particular areas, and we discussed newspaper advertising.

Mark didn't have a lot of money to spend over the year so we got copies of all the papers in the area (one regional, five local weekly, one free newsheet and an irregular publication from the local high school that went to the parents of the 700 children about every three months).

The first thing he did was create a list of questions for each publication about their circulation numbers and area, rates and discounts and what help the paper could give him in creating an ad (copywriting and graphics). Needless to say each of the papers told him that (1) they were the best in the area for what he wanted, and (2) he'd need to spend a lot more than he had planned.

However, ignoring that fine and no doubt unbiased advice, we took stock of the situation. The regional paper was too expensive and covered an area much bigger than Mark intended to cover. Of the five local weekly papers, only two had a good circulation and their rates were similar. The free newsheet was a pretty lousy publication but it did get delivered to every door in the exact area Mark wanted to cover.

Next he contacted a few advertisers from the papers to see what kind of response they had and took a few notes. Then he called the two good local papers again, told them they had quoted him the same rates, and gave them the opportunity to offer him more discount!

Finally, he decided to place a medium-sized ad in the one local weekly that gave him the best discount for twelve weeks, a big ad to make him stand out against the others in the free newsheet that would get him into every household for twelve weeks, and in every issue of the high-school paper which was only a few pounds and he felt would be a good PR exercise.

Only then did we get down to the work of creating his ad with the help of the folks at the weekly paper. They helped us put the ad together, but Mark used it in all the other papers too — another good saving!

Trade publications. There are hundreds of magazines on the shelves of every newsagent throughout the country. But for every magazine you see, there are three more that don't get put on shop shelves because they are specialist trade magazines and newspapers that are sold by subscription only. But even though they might have a small circulation and aren't read by the general public, these might be the perfect place for you, depending on your business.

For a lot of businesses the choice of advertising in trade publications will be obvious. For example, one of my clients imports specialist cheeses from around the world and sells to delicatessens, grocers and a number of hotels and restaurants. When we had a look at where he should spend his advertising budget we decided to place them in trade magazines and papers that are subscribed to by delicatessens, grocers and the catering trade — as far as you are concerned, this business doesn't exist. But his market is growing every year because he spends his advertising money where it works for him.

So do not ignore trade publications. Take time to go to your local library and have a look at what they might have available or contact local traders and ask them what magazines they subscribe to and try to get a look at them. If they're for you, begin to formulate a strategy for benefiting from them. Chances are they will be able to offer low advertising rates but if you decide they're not for you the only thing you've lost is a little research time.

2. *Radio advertising*

Nobody loves listening to the radio more than I do, but I only recommend it to a few of my clients for advertising. Not that radio advertising doesn't work. It does. But only if you have taken time to be very specific about your target market and you are 100 per cent certain that they listen to a particular radio station at particular times.

Unlike newspapers, radio listening figures are quite bogus when they are used to try and convince you that you should advertise with them. By definition, measurement of radio listeners is hit and miss even though the figures are released regularly and used as gospel by the radio ad salespeople.

Let me explain. A couple of times every year a poll is taken of listeners to radio stations. They are asked to monitor how many hours they spend listening to particular stations and at what times. These figures are then collated and made public and suddenly every station is number one: "the fastest growing station in this area", "the most listened to country and western station in the nation", "your first choice for talk radio". Every radio station can take the figures and, in all honesty, interpret them to their advantage.

The beauty of the whole thing is that you can tell exactly when these polls are about to be carried out because suddenly every station has upped their money give-aways from £100 to £1,000 every two minutes. Or you can win a brand new top-of-the-line BMW if you listen to station "A" every hour of the day for a week and answer three simple questions. A sudden burst of generosity on the part of the station management? Hardly. Simply an honest effort to manipulate the results of the polls.

So, the only way to advertise successfully on radio is to know absolutely positively certainly that your target audience will hear your ad. And the only way to do that is to ask them in your market research. And if you're determined to use radio advertising, then you need to use a bit of common sense in your dealings with the station.

If you sell office equipment and your local station has a business programme, then that's where you advertise, not on the mid-morning housewives' choice programme. If you sell Top 40 CDs and tapes then you advertise on a rock station that plays Top 40 tunes, not on your local talk-radio. If, on the other hand, your business is a corner store or a fruit shop or a fish and chip restaurant, I very much doubt if you could successfully and cost-effectively advertise on radio no matter how many people hear your ad.

This all sounds simple and obvious I know. But I also know how persuasive and tempting an ad salesperson can make their station sound. Hear them out, then think it out. Don't advertise just for the sake of it.

And a word of warning. If you decide to advertise on your local radio keep control of the process from beginning to end. Either write or at least review your own ad. Insist on choosing the voice that will present it. And know exactly when and how often your ad is going to go out. Do not under any circumstances allow the station to play the ad when they choose. Most stations will tempt you with an inexpensive package that gives them control over when the ad goes out. But unless you're trying to attract insomniacs who listen to rave music at 4:00 a.m., don't agree to it. It's your money, it's your ad, keep control.

Ann had a very nice little business in a small country town selling new and used books. Nothing too exciting, but enough to make it interesting. She did absolutely no advertising except for a mailing every November to known clients giving them three close-typed pages of her more interesting second-hand books in stock.

Then the ad salesman turned up. Apparently a new community radio station was opening in the next town which would cover a fairly wide area and they were looking for advertisers and sponsors. The programming was to cover a wide range of interests and the salesman assured Ann that an ad with them would "shoot her business through the roof". Little did he know, that that was the last thing she wanted. However, she was intrigued and said she would get back to him.

My wife and I were scheduled to have dinner with Ann and her husband Con, and over a lovely home-made casserole and fruity red wine (yes I can sometimes be bought by food and drink!), Ann brought up this visit. We all said that if she wanted to advertise there were many more effective ways of doing it than going blind onto an unknown and untested radio station. But she was insistent that she "give it a go", which is one of the most frightening terms a small business owner can use! It implies lack of research and no thought toward return on investment.

We argued back and forth, and finally I said, "All right. If this is something you want to do here's how you do it. Don't take an ad. Tell the salesman you'll come down to his station every Wednesday afternoon at 2:00 p.m. (Wednesday was half-day closing), and do a book review on a book of your choosing. The deal must be that the programme presenter mentions the name of your shop before and after your "slot", and you get to give the telephone number as well. And you'll give him a tenner for the privilege."

After a bit of thought Ann agreed that would be a good approach, called the station the next morning and after a bit of negotiation on the rate, has been a regular feature on Wednesday afternoons for the past two years. Her business hasn't "shot through the roof", but she does now provide a "book-search" and mail-order service which has made the weekly investment of time and money worthwhile.

4. Television advertising

David Ogilvy is recognised as an international guru of advertising. When he started his own advertising agency in New York in 1949 he expected to see advertising change time and time again during his career in the business. However, he now says that since 1949 there has only been one major change: "television has emerged as the most potent medium for selling most products."

And Ray Kroc, the founder of McDonald's, admitted that his business was going to the wall until he decided to throw everything he had into a few ads on a local Chicago television station and he never looked back.

So, there is no doubt that advertising on television is exciting and works. But it's also very expensive and you need to think long and hard before committing yourself to a TV campaign.

So, is TV advertising for you? Well, the real problem for Europeans is that even where you are dealing with what is referred to as a "local TV station", the chances are you are actually dealing with a regional one at best, and possibly even a national one. So, obviously TV ads will not be very cost effective if you're trying to convince people from 50 miles away to come and get their hair done in your beauty parlour!

On the other hand, if you operate a number of beauty parlours around the region or country, then you might be well served by TV ads. It's all a matter of common sense, your own judgement — and deep pockets!

5. Commercial telephone directories

As a means of having your name and number at hand for your customers, the commercial telephone directories (Yellow and Golden pages) are a must for all businesses. The only decision you have to make is how much to spend on the ad. If you're simply using the directory as a point of reference for people who already know your name but need your telephone number, then a one line entry will be enough. But if you're hoping to make potential customers pick up the telephone while their fingers are doing the walking, then you need an eye-catching ad and have to decide how much to spend.

A lot depends on your competition. If you are a florist, double glazing company or a coal man, for example, you'd better consider placing a good-sized, eye-catching ad because you're going to be fighting for attention on the page. On the other hand, if you're a specialist of some kind where there isn't a lot of competition, then a small ad with just a little detail of your service will do the trick.

The best way to decide is to look through your local pages and see what the competition is doing. In this instance they're going to help determine your own strategy.

Apart from the "official" telephone company directory there are a growing number of "local business" directories popping up all over the country. Once again, it's a judgement call as to whether or not you advertise with them. A rule of thumb would be if you do a lot of business by telephone then get into every directory going, otherwise think it through and measure each one on its merit.

6. Give-aways, gifts and gimmicks

Boy do people love these! I've just taken a quick look around my office and I have pens from my insurance man, a diary from the local travel agent, two pencils from a day out at the museum and a calendar from the Chinese take-away in town. And I'll bet you could create a similar list without too much difficulty. But before you go out and sink your entire budget into 5,000 personalised mugs ask yourself if giving things away will bring you customers. Frankly, I doubt it very much.

Give-aways, gifts and gimmicks do have their place in your advertising budget if you can stretch it to a few dozen of something. But please try to use your imagination when making your choice of what to order. The cleverest gimmick I've ever seen was a pencil that had been made in an "L"-shape with the message, "If this is the way your back feels it's time we talked" — Len Emery, Chiropractor. 555-1212. I've lost the pencil a long time ago, but I still remember the message. That's a gimmick that worked. So if you decide you would like to give things away to a few valued customers then take time to see what's available and try and find one that's relevant to your business and that'll work for you.

7. The back of the bus and other moving possibilities

Do you ever think that some people go into business just to have the opportunity of putting their names on anything that moves? I've seen advertising on the backs and sides of buses, inside taxis, in trains and even on couriers' bicycles. Now if you own a fleet of taxis or operate a courier company then I would encourage you to go out and persuade people to advertise with you. But I'm afraid I would not recommend that any of my clients take you up on the offer. Unless you've got a budget that stretches forever, I'd give this fine opportunity a miss. Lots of people would certainly see your ad on the back of a bus but how many of them are your target market? How many of them will be able to read your message as it flies past at 50 miles per hour? And how many will be quick enough to whip out paper and pencil to write down your telephone number before it disappears over the next hill? Not very many. Give this one a miss.

8. The internet

According to the computer whizzes, we will all be shopping and ordering services through the internet within the next few years. That's why there are all kinds of experts and consultants who are happy to separate you from £300+ to help you determine your "web site strategy".

Now, a quick look through the Internet will show you that there are a number of great opportunities on there for small businesses. If you're a craftsperson, for example, there are a number of "craft villages" available which can open up a world-wide market. Likewise there are quite a few service businesses on there so the Internet definitely can offer some businesses a potential market. But do be wary and take time to find out all you can about the possibilities.

There is a mountain of information available on the World Wide Web and the probability of somebody stumbling across your lone web site is slim. If you do want to get onto the Internet then take time to consult with somebody locally who knows all about it. A professional consultant will give you a lot of information at no charge to help you make your mind up, and they should be able to advise you on what "links" they will be able to provide for you (for example, if you're making pine furniture in a cottage in Wales, browsers would be able to find you listed under "pine furniture", "handmade furniture", "cottage industries" and "Welsh crafts" to name but a few. The more potential "links" you have the more you increase your chances of being found and upping your number of "hits" (the number of people who visit your site).

The Internet is a new and exciting opportunity for business owners, but don't allow yourself to be over-sold on the excitement. Keep the goal of high return for investment to the forefront and you'll be able to determine if this marketing method is for you at this time.

These are just a few thoughts on the most obvious advertising opportunities that you will find, but to note every possible advertising opportunity would take a full volume in itself! You'll have the opportunity to advertise on street maps, door-to-door drops, direct mail pieces and as many other ad spaces as there are ad salespeople to think of them.

Only select the ad opportunities that you can bet fairly well will work for you and use them extensively. Do not be tempted to go with the exotic or the downright weird as these will simply dilute your message and eat up your advertising budget.

What to spend

I will discuss how to set your budget in full later in the book, so the only thing I'll say for now is never, but never, pay the full amount your ad salesman quotes you. Always ask for discount whether it's for cash payment, an agreement to place ads for so many weeks or even because this is your first ad with their paper. Discounts are always available on advertising of any kind, and especially newspaper advertising, so make sure you get as much of a discount as you can. After all, the less you spend on this ad, the more often you'll be able to advertise, the more people will see your ads and the more business you will do. So it makes good business sense to squeeze the ad salesperson as much as possible. Believe me, if you have your cheque book in your hand, they won't lose the sale over a few pounds!

What to expect from your advertising

Expect success, great results, failure and despondency! That covers all possible results. The truth is, you really don't know what to expect from your advertising. A successful businessman once said to me, "I know that 50 per cent of my advertising works. If I only knew which 50 per cent I would save a fortune!"

And that's the simple truth of it. There are no guarantees in advertising and your job is to get the odds in your favour by carefully carrying out your market research and then taking time to decide on all of your advertising priorities knowing:

- What you want to achieve
- What you want to advertise
- Where to advertise it
- When to advertise it.

By doing the research and taking the time to make careful selections and decisions you can expect your advertising to work for you more often than not. But it is equally important to monitor the results and be prepared to change your approach when one seems to work better than another. Your task is to get your average well above the 50 per cent mark and you can only achieve that by carefully monitoring the results of, and reactions to, your advertising.

Advertising isn't an exact science, but with careful research, planning and monitoring, nor does it have to be a "shot in the dark".

TEN POINTS TO REMEMBER

1. Your ads must inform your market of your availability and persuade them to use you in preference to your competitors.

2. Before creating your ads you must think through your advertising priorities:

   • Make the cash register ring

   • Decide what you want to achieve from your ad

   • Decide what to advertise

   • Decide where to advertise

   • Decide when to advertise

   • Decide how to advertise.

3. Only place an ad when you are 100 per cent confident that your target market will see and respond to it, and that you will get an excellent return on your money.

4. Ad salesmen come armed with enough figures and statistics to boggle your mind. Hear them out, and then take time to think it out.

5. Don't dilute your budget or message by wasting money on the exotic or weird. Make your decisions and stick with them.

6. Be prepared to advertise for a set period of time before deciding whether an ad is working or not. One-off ads are seldom successful.

7. Only embark on an ad campaign if you can afford it. If you can't afford to advertise, start thinking about clever ways to promote your business.

8. Radio ads work and will be cost effective if you are absolutely sure your ad is being aired to your target market and you keep absolute control at all times.

9. TV advertising works. But it demands a high advertising spend and is only relevant if it is local to your business. TV advertising needs very careful thought.

10. You know your business and your customers better than anybody else. Be confident in your ability to reach them and only accept ad salesmen's advice and recommendations if it coincides with what you already know.

3

HOW TO BUDGET FOR ADVERTISING

And not break the bank!

How to choose a system of budgeting that best suits your business

Advertising is great. It's great for your business and it's great fun to do. But sometimes the excitement of the advertising becomes an end in itself and begins to get out of hand. When that happens your returns on your advertising do not justify the spending and you begin a downward spiral of spending more and more and getting less and less.

To prevent that from happening your advertising budget — just like any other budget in your business — must be carefully thought through. There are a number of ways to do that and we'll have a look at each of them. But in the end it will be entirely up to you which system you feel best meets the needs of your own business. Accept that you have to invest money to make money: choose the system which you feel is best for you, do the sums, decide on your budget and then stick to it. It will be tempting to overrun your ad budget more than any other, but in the end it will not be worth doing as your cash flow and profitability suffer.

1. The "I'll spend whatever it takes" system.

Here's a beauty. And if this is how you set your advertising budget I think it's time you took a look at your whole business structure. But it does happen. There are people who run their business on a month-to-month basis with no thought to strategic planning. If they've had a good month this month, they'll spend a bit more on advertising next month. And the same approach goes for a bad month. There is the temptation to buy advertising on the hoof without any thought to the "buying cycle" or the realities of their business. And there is no thought to a final figure at the end of the year.

At best, businesses that employ this method of advertising will be very popular with advertising sales at their local newspapers and might even have a few hits with their advertising. But at worst they will be throwing money away as they buy an ad here and there without any thought to strategy, overall cost or monitoring for results.

2. The "I'll spend whatever the other boys are spending" system.

Nobody will tell you to keep an eye on your competitors more than I will. Get to know what they're up to and watch every new twist to their strategy to keep ahead.

But I would never in a million years suggest that you let them determine your advertising/marketing strategy. And if you choose to react to your competitors' advertising, cut prices, sales, offers and overall approach to marketing, then you are letting them determine your marketing approach.

And yet it's very easy to do, especially if your competition is a lot bigger than you are. If they're doing something then it's probably the right thing and it's a lot easier for you to react to their lead.

I appreciate that, but I can tell you that it won't work. You will be forever in their shadow and will never be able to develop a plan for yourself. So, if I were advising you, I would want you to begin developing a strategy of your own. Always keep an eye on the competition and where necessary react to something they're doing, but for the most part, develop your own marketing plan and stick with it. Make yourself different to the other guy because there is a good chance that he is simply running on the seat of his pants without market research or any concept of what his customers really want.

Set your own strategy and stick with it. Do not allow yourself to be lead by how others run their business — ever!

3. The "I'll spend 3 per cent of gross sales on advertising" system.

This is the easiest way to determine your advertising budget. It's simple, it doesn't need a great amount of calculation or accounting, and it ensures a certain amount of money is available for adverting on a monthly basis.

It's also about as flexible as a concrete brick. What if you need to take a little chance and spend a bit more to boost sales in an unexpectedly quiet time? This system doesn't let you do it.

It looks great and it sounds great, but the reality is something entirely different as the market ebbs and flows and does not really take much notice of easy formulae for solving problems or meeting demands.

4. The "Let's sit down and think it through" system.

As you can imagine, this is my choice and the one I use with my clients. It takes into account the realities of the business and its "buying cycle", the cost of advertising in the local media, and the available funds. Put them all together, mix them up a bit, make provision for a "crisis fund" and I think you'll come up with a system that works for just about any business big or small.

Here's how it works:

1. On a large piece of squared paper write out all of the different types of advertising you intend to employ during the year (newspaper ads, brochures, direct mail, radio ads, in-store promotions, fliers, etc.). Along the top put the months of the year. This will now be your Advertising Budget Master Page. Take 12 pieces of ordinary lined paper and title each one January, February, March, etc.

2. On the 12 pieces of paper write down what you would plan to do to advertise your business in full and in each of the categories as listed on the Master Page. At this stage you will have to take into account what you know, or think, to be seasonal highs

and lows, your business's buying cycle and influences such as the weather and other influences on your day-to-day sales.

3. Having completed this lengthy process, estimate as closely as possible how much each of these elements of your advertising are going to cost and enter the figures — in pencil — on the Master Page.

4. Add up the costs monthly and for an overall cost for the year.

5. Pick yourself back up off the floor again!

6. Begin to revise your plan month-by-month moving things around, cutting some back or out completely and mixing it all up a bit until you have a plan that will achieve most of your advertising goals at a cost figure you can live with.

7. Put your plan into action.

8. Monitor your plan month-to-month being prepared to amend and change, add and take away where necessary. Most importantly, be prepared to react to any situation that might occur that means a drastic change in your plan. For example, you might have to react to something your competitors do that will mean taking a greater bite at the budget over a two or three month period. Do you decide to add that cost into your budget, or can you save money by shaving a bit off in ensuing months? It's your decision but if you have everything on paper and are continually monitoring and "tweaking" the plan where necessary, you'll be in control of the situation at all times.

This system is a bit of all of the others brought together and added to instinct and business knowledge. There always have to be allowances made for knowledge and the unexpected when creating budgets and I believe they should always be fluid rather than determined and struck in stone never to be revised or reviewed. The most important thing is to keep your advertising spending within acceptable limits, but allowing for those limits to be fairly movable in the course of the year.

If you're having a particularly bad season or year you might decide to tighten your belt in all areas including advertising. On the other hand, you might calculate that by boosting your advertising you can lift sales enough to make it worthwhile. There is no way a book can tell you which one to do. Only you as the owner of the business can take time to monitor the situation on a daily basis and draw your own conclusions from what you see and experience.

TEN POINTS TO REMEMBER

1. You must speculate to accumulate. Advertising is a financial necessity that requires its own budget.

2. Your advertising must not become an end in itself. It must create enough business to be justified.

3. Once you've decided which system of budgeting to adopt, stick with it and see it through. If you decide to change, then be prepared to take time to change it completely and positively.

4. Your marketing/advertising plan needs to be prepared with your business in mind, not as a reaction to your competition.

5. You need a long-term (12 month) advertising strategy. Planning and budgeting month-to-month is a recipe for failure and wasted money and opportunities.

6. Your advertising spending must reflect your customers' "buying cycle". No amount of advertising will convince your customers to buy great amounts of coal in the summer.

7. Using a percentage of gross sales to determine your advertising budget is easy to do, but inflexible. Is this the right system for your business? Does it allow you to react to unforeseen circumstances?

8. Take time to think through your advertising goals and priorities before finalising your advertising budget.

9. Write your advertising budget in pencil. You're going to have to change it regularly!

10. Monitor your advertising. If something is not working, then be prepared to remove it from your budget. Likewise, if it is working beyond your highest hopes, then be prepared to amend your budget to funnel more money into this form of advertising.

4

HOW TO WRITE A WINNING DIRECT MAIL CAMPAIGN

The small business owner's most powerful secret weapon!

What is direct mail?

We should first establish that there is a difference between "direct mail" and "mail order".

Mail order is a fabulous way to make money. You advertise your service or product (usually product) heavily in the media. Then you sit back and wait for the orders and cheques to arrive in your mail box.

At least that's what all the "how to get rich in mail order" books say. In my experience it's a bit more difficult than that, although the theory is basically the same.

Direct mail, on the other hand, is one of the weapons in the marketing arsenal of all small businesses. Well, actually, it's not just one more weapon in the arsenal. If used properly, direct mail is the most powerful, cost-effective and exciting advertising you and your business will ever experience. No matter whether you're a retailer or wholesaler, importer or exporter, established or new, in a high-street premises or battling for your financial life in the back bedroom, direct mail is the one method of advertising that you can depend on to boost your business quickly and effectively if, in order of importance:

1. You've got a mailing list of excellent prospects.

2. You've got a product/service those prospects want.

3. You can make them an offer they'll find irresistible.

With a little time and energy spent on research, you will be able to create a Winning Direct Mail Campaign that could very easily *double your sales.*

   And if that introduction hasn't got your attention, then I'm in the wrong business!

Why I think your business must use direct mail

So many business people I talk to say:

> "Oh yeah, direct mail. It's great for the big boys, but I'm just a small shopkeeper (retailer, service-supplier, garage owner, mechanic, etc. etc.). It wouldn't do me any good. My customers wouldn't respond to it and would probably think it's just more junk mail."

Well here are two interesting facts for you: (1) the smaller your business the more effective direct mail becomes, and (2) the smaller your business, the more cost-effective direct mail is.

   It makes sense, doesn't it? If you're a small business with a catchment area of a mile and your local paper covers an area of 20 miles, how much are you spending to advertise to people who won't ever come near your town let alone your business?! Instead, if you took the £75 you were going to spend on an ad and sent letters directly to people who you know use your business, wouldn't that be more effective?

And while we're on the subject, let me tell you that there is absolutely no such thing as "junk mail". It's a useless term bandied about by people who aren't in touch with the modern world. The mail has always been a superb method for getting information from a business to a consumer and every piece of mail that hits your doormat brings with it knowledge of some sort and can't be called "junk". And certainly the direct mail you're going to send (notice I didn't say might send) is going to give your customers or potential customers some real information that will be of great benefit to them and which they will not consider to be "junk mail".

Unlike any other form of advertising, direct mail goes directly to the people you want to reach. It doesn't have to compete for space on the page of the newspaper and you aren't paying for it to be read by hundreds (possibly thousands) of people that don't really care about you or your business.

And unlike any other form of advertising, direct mail is completely controllable to the point of being able to pinpoint exactly where you have succeeded and exactly where you have failed, and will let you react appropriately. If you send out 100 letters and get 10 responses then you have a 10 per cent response rate. If your letters cost you £35 to post and every sale netted you £10 then you would know that mail-shot had brought £65 profit into your business (£100 income – £35 costs = £65 profit). Plus you would now have 10 customers who could be depended on to respond to a mail shot in the future.

Will you take the "100 Letter Challenge"?

But you're probably still thinking that your business is different. That your customers are different to every other consumer in the world and so wouldn't respond to a mail shot from you. But they would. And I'll prove it to you if you accept my "100 Letter Challenge" to post only 100 letters and monitor your response.

Follow the steps to a Winning Direct Mail Campaign closely, send your letters and then call me with the results. No matter what business you're in if your mailing meets the three important criteria at the beginning of the chapter and you follow each step as we go along you will be amazed at the way your customers respond. That's how confident I am that direct mail is a good advertising choice for your business, whatever it is.

And even if you're just considering starting a business you should make provision for direct mail in your budget. If you're at the stage of putting the final touches on your business plan, then sharpen your pencil again and jiggle your figures to give yourself a budget for direct mail. If you've done your market research properly, there is no better, faster and more effective way to get your message to your potential customers than by direct mail. Spend every penny you have on other media if you want, but you'll be making a mistake if you don't earmark some of your advertising budget on direct mail.

But there is a snag with direct mail. If you go to a newspaper and say you want to spend £300 on advertising they'll sit down and help you write your ad and may even illustrate it for you. Same if you go to a radio station and throw money at them. But there isn't anybody to help with your direct mail. It's a lonely old business that you have to motivate yourself to do and make the time to do it in. So here's what you do:

1. Decide you're going to do a mailing of just 100 to see how it works

2. Adapt the steps below to your business to come up with a mailer you're happy with

3. Monitor the results

4. Do it again!

Getting started

Like everything else, getting started with your campaign is the most important and difficult thing to do. You've decided you want to try direct mail, but where do you begin?

There are three points that you must have very clearly defined: (1) what are you trying to achieve from your direct mail campaign? (2) who is your target market? and (3) what can you offer them that will be appealing enough to make them buy?

1. Setting your goals

Well, let's start at the end. Let's start by deciding what you want to achieve from your mailing. And let's make that something easily measurable. For example, deciding "I want to get some more customers" is important, but a little vague. Instead you might decide "I want to boost my sales by 5 per cent during the next quarter" or "I want to get 5 more regular customers" or "I want to sell my last 10 garden gnomes."

Whatever you decide you want to achieve through your direct mail make it realistic and make it measurable. Expect great things from your direct mail campaign, but don't expect the world. Here are three things that direct mail can do for your business:

1. Bring in new customers

2. Increase the "per-visit" spend from existing customers

3. Increase the number of times existing customers buy from you.

Which one is right for you? If you're a new business you'll certainly want to bring new customers to your business. And I haven't yet come across any businessperson who wouldn't appreciate a higher spend or more regular visits from their existing customers.

It's also important to have a clear view of what you're trying to achieve to keep a focus on the actual mailing. It is very easy to just sit down and start writing a letter that doesn't actually ask your customer to use your business more often or spend more money! It is possible for you to write a three page letter filled with so many offers and encouragements that you'll actually turn your customers off.

Get focused on what you want to achieve, and then discipline yourself to keep to it.

2. Defining your target market

Next you need to decide who you're writing to. The most effective list is known customers, people who have already used your service or bought in your shop. But if you're just getting your new business together and don't have such a list there are numerous places to find names and addresses and we will discuss those later.

What you want to achieve will very much influence who you're writing to. If you're promoting a sale or a new service, for example, you'll write to existing customers. But if you want to achieve a greater customer base then you'll write to people who aren't your customers yet but who have the same characteristics as your existing customers.

Or you might use your existing customers to bring you new ones. I live by the sea and the nearest town has a fairly well established fishing tackle shop. One day Bob, the owner, was chatting to me as I looked through his latest catalogue. He said many of his customers had matured with him and he wasn't getting too many new customers into the shop. His greatest fear was that one day he'd wake up and find they'd buried his last customer!

As I whiled away a lazy afternoon hanging off the end of the harbour, I thought over his problem and we arranged to get together to discuss it later in the week.

Now I knew that Bob had a good mailing list because he sent out catalogues to his regular customers. But I also knew that — even though he really wanted more customers — he wouldn't want to spend a lot of money on some fancy list from a mailing house. It might give him so many thousand "known fishermen" in his area, but frankly the list would cost too much and many of the names would be irrelevant.

So we chatted and decided to use his existing customers as the way to get new ones. And we decided to do it by direct mail.

First we decided what we wanted to achieve. If we sent 200 letters Bob wanted 20 new customers. A 10 per cent response! It was a high expectation, but we knew we had a really good list and went with it.

Then we decided who we would write to. Bob had a list of almost 300 but many of them lived a distance away and only came to him in the summer when they were on holiday so we removed them and a few others and ended up with a list of 192 names and addresses.

Finally we created the mailing piece itself. It would include the catalogue, a personal letter from Bob saying thanks for their custom in the past and reminding them of his commitment to get his hands on any specific fishing tackle they required, and then asked them to bring a friend along next time they were visiting the shop. And to "encourage" them to do so Bob said they would get £1 off every purchase they made for every £10 their friend spent. What's more, their friend could also enjoy £1 off anything over £10. Two appropriate vouchers were included in the mailing.

So now nearly 200 known customers had the latest catalogue of their favourite fishing gear to whet their appetites and a golden opportunity to save money off every bit of it for no effort!

Wow! This was a very strong piece of direct mail, and of course it worked. Over the next 8 weeks in the lead up to the season, customers, their friends, their sons and grandsons literally flocked to Bob's shop. It was quite phenomenal and he measured his response at a whopping 25 per cent!

Now let's not get carried away here. This was a fantastic response but it wasn't without cost. Bob had to send out almost 200 letters and give the equivalent of 20 per cent off a lot of his stock in what was traditionally a busy time of the year for him — early spring. But the long-term payoff was well worth it. He achieved his immediate goal by bringing in a lot of new customers, and he achieved his long-term goal by making sure he kept them and got his initial investment back many times.

His response was brilliant and it was because he had fulfilled the three criteria for a Winning Direct Mail Campaign:

1. A super mailing list

2. A product they wanted

3. An offer they couldn't refuse.

3. What are you going to write to get the response you need?

Many people find this the most difficult part of the whole process, but it shouldn't be. The most important, yes, the most difficult, no. Simply write the letter as you would write to a friend. After all, these are your customers. You probably know them by first name and know a bit about their family. So get a picture of one of your favourite customers in your mind's eye and write to them.

Keep it simple, friendly and to the point. No big words or fancy phrases. No clever puns or convoluted ideas. You're writing to a friend that you want to come and visit you, not a solicitor who is going to dissect every word.

How to create a mailing list that'll get results

There are three ways of creating a mailing list. One is to go to a direct mail specialist who will "do a search" of special and exclusive lists that only professionals have access to. A list that will be "tailor made" to your particular needs and will give you the best potential customers based on your "lifestyle profile". I don't favour small businesses using these folks because they're often too expensive and not very helpful for a small, localised company. But if you're looking for a wider audience, or if you're selling something very specialised, then this is definitely the place to start. To find a direct mail specialist near you start by looking at the Yellow Pages under — you guessed it — direct mail.

The second is to get a hold of somebody else's mailing list. Somebody whose customers have a similar lifestyle to your own customers. If you're selling golf carts, for example, you might be able to rent the membership list of some golf clubs at a price. Lists are available everywhere from magazines, papers, charities, and just about anybody that has a mailing list will be happy to rent their list to you. It can be a bit expensive, but if you're convinced their list will work for you, then it's money well spent.

Or you can create your own list, which is what I would recommend. In fact you probably have a mailing list right now.

No? What about a list of people you've done service calls for? What about the customers that have accounts with you? What about the layaway customers, the Christmas Club members, the people who filled in your questionnaire when you were doing your market research?

These aren't just lists of names, these are mailing lists. And I'll bet if you sat down with a sheet of paper you could come up with a lot more names of customers right now. Don't know their address? What about checking it in the phone book? Know the street but not the number? Check the electoral register at the library.

And start getting more addresses right now, today. Find some way to get as many names and addresses of your customers as possible and get them onto the list.

Get creative! A pizza chain I did some work for offered a delivery service. What happened to every name and address of delivery customers? You're right, they went on the mailing list. So when the owner realised that the vast majority of his customers ordered pizza on the weekend leaving his midweek staff under utilised he decided to do something about it. Using his mailing list of people he knew used his service, he sent them a personal letter offering them a 12" pizza for the price of a 9" on mid-week nights. Result: many of his customers started having pizza twice a week!

And I love to tell the story of the shoe shop owner who became obsessed with the idea of doing direct mail. When he thought of the number of different seasons and ranges he could offer he knew he could get customers back into his shop to spend money a few times a year.

He didn't have a mailing list of any sort but when he heard that the local hospital was to close he immediately got a petition form on his counter and had everybody who came into his shop — whether they bought or not — sign the petition and give their address. Hey presto! Instant mailing list of people who were prepared to consider using his shop when they were looking for shoes! Plus he got some free PR when he added his petition to others around town.

And just because you're working from home, or haven't even started your business yet, doesn't mean you don't have a mailing list. Just look in the Yellow Pages or any other directory relevant to your business, and you'll find a list.

But if you really don't have a list of any kind, then it's time to look at the characteristics of your customers and see if others of the same type are available for you to create a list for.

Our window cleaner was trying to develop his business and asked me if I knew anybody who wanted to get their windows cleaned. Now I'm all for asking for referrals but it can result in travelling all over the country if your customers haven't been thoughtful enough to make friends with their neighbours. So I said to him "Listen, Fred what you need is a bit of direct mail." And what did he say? "Oh. I couldn't afford that . . . it's for the big boys . . . my customers wouldn't respond to it."

So I set him my "100 Letter Challenge". I asked him to decide which was his busiest area and then go to the library and look up the electoral register for those streets and get a copy of the names and addresses.

Then we wrote a very simple letter:

**Fred Smith
Window cleaner**

Dear Mrs O'Brien,

**For less than 50p a day I can keep your
windows sparkling.**

There's nothing worse than coming home from work, relaxing in your favourite chair and looking out of the window only to realise it's time to clean them again!

But not any more. For only £3 a week I'll clean every window in your house upstairs and down. No more dirt or streaks. Just sparkling windows.

I'm in your area every Wednesday and can add you to my list of calls from next week. Simply call me and leave a message on the machine if necessary.

Thanks,

Fred

PS Call me by Friday of this week and I'll be happy to offer you an extra special "New Customer Price" of £2 for the first week.

Nothing fancy. Just a good offer of service and price. And to save more money Fred hand-delivered the letters himself. No sooner had he delivered his 100 letters than he had 3 calls and 3 new customers which rose to 7 in the first week. Over the following month 5 other people stopped him and asked him to do their windows as well. A total of 12 new customers and £36 per week for an initial outlay of less than £10 plus a little time! As you can imagine, it didn't take a lot of convincing to get Fred back to the library for his next 100 letters.

So don't let cost or apparent lack of a list get in your way. Be imaginative and get your list as good as possible. Every good qualified name means potential sales. Every poor unqualified name means costs.

How to write letters that'll get more people buying more from you more often

Now you know what you want to achieve from your campaign and who you're writing to to get those results. It's time to write the letter, to create a masterpiece of copy. Scary, isn't it? Get out a clean white sheet of paper and a pen and try to write a letter that'll knock their socks off right now and you'll sit for a long time.

Before you think of writing a complete letter from scratch, it's much easier if you think of it as individually important different elements which come together to make one effective whole:

- The headline
- The body of the letter
- The PS
- The inclusions
- The envelope.

Each are important and do a separate job and I think the best way to illustrate how each works is to create an example. The specifics of this letter might be different to your own, but the theory and the practice will be exactly the same. Approach your own letter the same way, and you are guaranteed to have exactly what you're looking for — honestly!

Our client is a small 14-room hotel set in a coastal town about 40 miles away from the nearest city. They have been in business for about 10 years and have a great reputation for service. They have no fancy restaurant, leisure centre or entertainment on site, but they do have a very relaxing atmosphere and the owner encourages his staff to make guests feel like "family" visiting for a day or two.

It's now near the end of summer and the autumn/winter business is looking pretty bleak. Three years ago the owner put in a computerised reservation system and has access to a full list of every person who has stayed in the hotel in that time. As he doesn't have a big budget for advertising — and frankly wouldn't know where to spend it anyway as his guests come from all over the country — he's decided to use direct mail.

His overall goal is to achieve a 35 per cent occupancy rate with an average per person spend of £35 per night dinner, bed and breakfast from October 1 to December 24 — a twelve-week period. That's around 400 room nights @ £70 per room (£35 x 2 people) = £28,000 in turnover.

Based on past figures he can expect around 200 room nights booked over the twelve weeks, and wants the same again from his direct mail.

Sifting through his files he creates a list of 1,000 names which he feels are good qualified customers and he's going to offer them a special rate for a two-night "Mini Break". So before we've even considered writing his letter we have done our research, defined our market and set our goals.

From a mailing of 1,000 letters to known clients we are expecting 100 two-night reservations to return £14,000 in revenue. A 10 per cent response is required if we are to be completely successful and we have fulfilled the three criteria for a Winning Direct Mail Campaign:

- We've got a good qualified list of known clients

- We've got a product we know they like

- We've got an offer we believe they'll go for.

So here's the letter and simple "inclusion" we're going to send everybody on the list:

The Mariner's Inn
Anytown

Dear Mr Smith,

**For only £34.50 you can enjoy another memorable
break in the relaxing and friendly atmosphere
of The Mariner's Inn.**

I'm sitting here looking over the water as the seagulls wheel low in a sky orange from a beautiful setting sun. It really is a superb sight, and I thought I would write to invite you back to enjoy it with us again this year.

We are so lucky living in this quiet corner of the country. As you know, the days are long and lazy and time seems to drift past when you're here. It's a bit of a surprise, then, to realise that the summer is almost over and the crisp clean evenings of autumn are just around the corner. In fact, we just got our first delivery of logs yesterday and it won't be long before you'll be welcomed back from a walk on the beach to the wonderful smell of an open fire.

So won't you join us for a day or two? We've completely redecorated your room and we hope you'll enjoy the warm relaxing colours we've chosen. And you'll find Chef Bernie's cuisine to be a pleasure — as always!

Because we'd love to have you back again, we have put together a two-day package for you to take advantage of anytime between October 1 and December 21. For only £34.50 per person per night, you can enjoy two relaxing nights with us, two wonderful breakfasts to set you up for a day's walking or reading, and two 4 course dinners in the "Captain's Rest" with a full choice of anything on the menu (including Bernie's famous seafood salad).

That's two nights in a beautiful en suite room, two full cooked breakfasts, and two 4 course dinners in the "Captain's Rest" for only £69 per person!

It's almost "two" good to be true!

Mr Smith, I look forward to personally welcoming you back to The Mariner's Inn. If there's any way that any of us here can be of assistance, please don't hesitate to call.

Regards,

Alex Carruthers

PS Make your reservation before October 1st and I'll be pleased to have a complementary chilled bottle of champagne in your room awaiting your arrival.

(Pre-printed back of a postcard of the hotel to be included with letter):

Dear

We thought you might like to join us for a couple of days at The Mariner's Inn. Because we're valued guests we can bring you along at the special rate of only £69 per person which includes two nights bed and breakfast and two superb dinners in the "Captain's Rest".

We're going to book for two nights from

_____(dates)

If you come with us not only will we both have a bottle of champagne waiting for us in our rooms from the owner, but we'll also get a FREE pre-dinner drink each evening. Do call and say you'll come!

Regards,

To be sure you have created a Winning Direct Mail Campaign every element of your letter must be given special attention.

1. How to write a headline that makes them stop in their tracks

Here's the assumption everybody in involved with direct mail should make: your customer picks up your letter from the doormat and starts making their way back to the bin which is in the kitchen. Your letter has a potential life span of 10-15 seconds unless you can get their attention about half way down the hall!

Your headline has got to make them stop and draw them into the letter giving you the opportunity to "make your pitch". So, rule number one is, always start with an eye-catching headline. Over 90 per cent of the people who receive your letter will read the headline and you need to convince a high percentage of them that what you have to offer is good enough to take their valuable time to find out about.

In our example headline we've made our pitch early remembering who our audience is. These people have used our product and just the mention of it will conjure up pictures and feelings so we capitalise on that immediately. We could have been a lot more blatant with something like "We're giving the hotel away!" But that's both crass and completely unbelievable and is therefore an advertising no-no.

There are no formulas for success in direct mail but each section of your letter can benefit from the experience and mistakes of others so here are some observations about your headline to consider:

- It must either offer an immediate benefit to the reader, or create curiosity in what you have to offer.

- It must make the reader stop and say, "Yes, I want to know more about why this person has written to me".

- It must be credible. If your customer doesn't believe what you're saying in your letter you can bet they won't trust what you say in person either. Your headline has to say something to your customers; it doesn't have to yell in their ear.

Certain words get people's attention too, and this applies to all advertising headlines, not just direct mail. They might seem like clichés and overused tired words, but they're used so much because they work.

Glamorous	Outperforms	Heart-thumping
Made to last	Stunning	Exclusive
Secret	Vital	Whopping
Proven	Genuine	Smashing
Elegant	Competitive	Confidential
Golden	Experienced	Sexy
Best-selling	Distinguished	Word of mouth
Sparkle	Treasure chest	Lucrative
Last minute	Take action now	Breakthrough

Every one of these words or phrases offer a benefit or raise curiosity. You can probably think of others so don't be afraid to use words that seem overused. The idea is to get their attention and get results, not spend hours trying to come up with creative words and phrases that won't be appreciated and will cost you money you can't afford.

Here are a few headlines that have worked:

- How to win friends and influence people

- The lazy man's way to riches

- Does the way you dress say something about you?

- This is your last chance to save money

- Order today and get my FREE booklet on how to make extra money in your spare time.

- Is the life of a child worth £1 per month to you?

When you come up with one that gets people's attention as well as these do I'd like to hear about them.

2. How to write a letter that gets their fingers dialling your number

Everything between the headline and your signature is called the "body copy" of your letter. It's where you make your pitch for the business. Its job is to give the reader enough reasons to buy your product or service. It has to convince them that yours is the service or product they want and it has to get them to make a buying decision within a specific time frame — preferably today!

In our example letter, the body copy takes a very soft-sell approach. We're not trying to sell second-hand cars here, we're trying to persuade people that they deserve a break and remind them what the product is like.

We've taken a very personal approach in this letter and it works well. The hotelier knows his customers and he wanted to convey the idea that he was thinking of them personally when he looked out over the water. And later in the letter he could just as easily have said "we've renovated all the rooms". But how much more personal to say "we've completely redecorated *your* room".

In short, the letter was written to the needs and desires of the reader, not the writer. If your letter is to be successful you must not be tempted to simply list all of the great attributes of your product or service without being sure to tell the reader what each one will do for him.

WII-FM. Murray Raphael is a well respected master of direct mail and he knows that even though there are many radio stations throughout the country, every one of your customers and mine are tuned in to one particular station. It's called "WII-FM" and when your customers read your ad or letter they tune right in to that station. WII-FM: "**What's In It For Me?**"

Nobody is going to buy your product based on its specifications unless they are relevant to them. So your job in the body of your letter is to show as many benefits as possible for using your product/service. By the time the reader reaches your signature you've got to have them wondering how they've ever managed to get this far without whatever it is you're offering!

So when you're writing your body copy keep a list of the "features and benefits" of your service or product beside you and write them into the letter.

- "Now we stock long-handled shovels (feature) so your back will never be strained again (benefit)."

- "We buy our widgets direct from the factory (feature) and pass the savings straight to you (benefit)."

Let your reader know that there's something in this for them, some tangible benefit that's going to fulfil a need or want and get some action.

The "Y" word. The words "you" and "your" are used 16 times in the example letter. It is probably impossible to overuse the word "you" in your letter and you should aim to get your "you count" high. In fact, once you've written your first draft go through and circle every "I" or "we" and see how many of them you can change to "you" by slightly reconstructing the sentence. Your whole letter will change its emphasis and your readers will know that you're writing to include them personally and not simply to blow your own horn.

So keep your letter personal, simple and direct. Don't try to oversell and don't make claims that are unbelievable. Write as many words as you have to, but no more than you need. The length of your letter is relatively unimportant but you must tell your customer enough to get them to take action.

3. *How to make your PS a powerful tool*

I shouldn't think too many of us have taken time to analyse how we actually read a letter. It seems pretty obvious that you start at the beginning and go through to the end. But according to the results of scientific tests done in Scandinavia in the 1980s, nothing could be further from the truth.

Using all sorts of fancy technology that neither you nor I need to understand, they discovered that the first stop for your eye is at any outstanding points at the top of the letter. That's why a headline in bold letters or a different font makes its impact.

Then your eye goes straight to the bottom to see who the letter is from. And while it's there it reads the PS before even going anywhere near the body copy. So that's why I emphasise the importance of both your headline and PS. They are the gateways to your letter.

PS's are so important that I always make sure I have two points in them. The first is another reason to buy and the second is a "call to action". In the example letter we've said you'll get a free bottle of champagne (the

extra reason to buy), but only if you book by October
1st (the "call to action"). So before the reader even begins reading the body of the letter he knows he's going
to get a great deal at a hotel he loves and get a free bottle of champagne if he acts quickly.

These are the highlights, the bullet points. Now we
can use the body of the letter to tease out the message
even more. But in the short time from doormat to bin
we can be confident that the reader has a good idea of
exactly what we have to offer. Enough to let him decide
to keep the letter, read it thoroughly and then get on
the phone!

That's the point of the PS. If you're selling a service
the same theory applies. Your PS should include an
extra feature of your service and then add a "call to action" which might include a relevant product. For example:

> "PS: Arrange to have a no-obligation financial
> review with one of our agents by November
> 15th and you'll also get a FREE pocket calcula-
> tor."

The calculator is relevant to the service and an added
incentive to make the appointment.

No matter what business yours is, a letter with a
strong PS that offers an extra benefit and a call to action
has a much higher chance of being read and acted upon
than one without.

4. How to give them another reason to buy more

If you've ever received a direct mail piece from the
Readers' Digest or one of many other companies, you'll

probably wonder why there are so many pieces of paper along with the main sales letter. And if you've ever tried to complete the paperwork needed to get into the final round of some major cash prize you'll know you have to read the letter three or four times to get all the information you need to complete the entry form. Which means, of course, that you also have to read all about the product being sold three or four times as well. Clever stuff.

I'm going to assume your budget won't stretch to five different glossy brochures printed to be included with your letter and that you don't intend to get your readers to peel off labels and numbers to claim £250,000 in cash.

But I am going to assume that you do want to make your mailer as successful as possible and so I'm going to recommend that you do have a second piece with your main letter. It doesn't have to be complicated, but it does have to either supplement or compliment your main offer.

In this mailer we've cleverly included a postcard which allows the recipient to invite a friend along at the same price. Now what's the advantage? Well, actually there are two: first we're building our chances of getting two rooms — and maybe even more — booked instead of one, and equally important we've made the reader feel he's a part of something. Now he can go to his friends and offer *them* something they can't get anywhere else because he's special and in the know. We've given him an opportunity to build his ego a bit, and who doesn't like that now and again?

Ten more ways to guarantee yours will be a winning direct mail piece

The way your letter looks will actually determine its success. An easy to read letter written in an informal way will be read by more people than a page crammed with big words and complex sentences. So it pays to take time to create a letter that looks well and reads easily. There are no hard and fast rules in direct mail, any more than there are with any type of advertising, but here are 10 ways to lay out your letter that will help ensure a higher proportion of your readers stay with you right through to the end.

1. Leave lots of "white space" around the copy. Wide margins, short paragraphs and lots of empty space top and bottom of the page.

2. Forget most of the rules you learned in your English classes. Obviously you don't want to use bad grammar, but it's OK to start sentences with "and" and "but". And it's OK to use everyday language and even clichés if they work for you. You should write your letter in the same way as you would talk to your customer. Worry more about the content than the structure of the sentences.

3. Use short sentences. Read your letter out loud when you're finished and if you have to stop to take a breathe half way through a sentence, it's too long!

4. Don't use long words when short ones will do the trick.

5. When you've drafted your letter take a red pen and circle every "I" and exaggerated claim you've

made. Then change them to "you" or "your" and believable claims.

6. Keep everything simple. Keep your goal in sharp focus and be careful not to wander off into irrelevancies in your letter. Remember KISS: **Keep It Simple, Stupid**

7. And while we're remembering acronyms, remember that the goal of your letter to achieve AIDA:

    -   Grab their **Attention**

    -   Hold their **Interest**

    -   Create a **Desire**

    -   Get them to take **Action**

8. Don't get carried away by the discovery of new "fonts". Fonts are the different typesetting styles available to you and modern day computers and commercial printers have access to hundreds of different ones. In fact the computer I'm working on at the moment has 167 different fonts! It's OK to use different fonts in your letter to highlight certain things, but never use more than 3 in any one letter or you'll lose your reader. For example, if I were to start changing my fonts all **of** a sudden, you **would** begin **to lose** interest **in** WHAT I had **TO SAY** and try to figure out what I was up to! The same with your readers. They don't want to be impressed with your font selection, they want to find out how what you have will benefit them.

9. Always, but always, print your letter in black type on white paper and sign your name with blue ink.

Don't get into reverse print (black background with white type), paper that's half white and half coloured, green ink or — worst of all — using paper with a picture on it and then overprinting your message. Make your message as clear and easy to read as possible.

10. Make it easy for your customers to respond to your offer. Include simple return cards if you have to, but let them use the phone to buy if possible. If you take credit cards say so and encourage your customer to use them. Don't make your customers jump through hoops to get your service or product because they won't do it. They might love what you have to offer, but unless they can respond easily they won't bother. Your letter will join the "must do" pile which is the one right before the "shred this" pile!

How to get them to open your envelope

If your customers don't open your envelope then all of your work thus far has been a waste of time! The bad news is that there is no sure-fire way to get people to open envelopes of any kind. The good news is there are some tricks that can get the odds in your favour.

After everything I've sad about black on white being your only choice for letters, here's the exception. Coloured envelopes stand out from the others on the doormat. So if you can get coloured envelopes at prices that won't break the budget then use them.

Should you overprint your envelopes with a "teaser" of some sort? Well, definitely, maybe, yes, perhaps, no, definitely not. Pick whichever one suits you best! In the balance I would say no because it's hard to justify the cost and coming up with something that will not actually be a turn-off is very difficult. As soon as you print something on your envelope other than a re-turn address it's a dead-give-away that what's inside is a circular of some kind. So unless you're absolutely sure what you're about to print on your envelope is going to be a winner, give it a miss.

Hand write the main address. Boy, do people hate when I suggest this one! But let's think about it first. Imagine you've a pile of mail in front of you. There are a couple of brown envelopes, two white ones with windows, two white ones that have labels or have been typed and one white one that has your name and ad-dress hand-written. Which one do you open first? Which one promises to be the most personal and there-fore the most positive experience? The hand-written one — every time!

If your mailing list is 1–200 then this is a tedious but not too time-consuming effort. More than 200 and it becomes impossible. Then I suggest you find a font that resembles handwriting as closely as possible. On the example envelope at the end of this chapter I've used a font called "Brush Script". I'm not sure if it's the best one available, but it's the best I've got on this computer.

Nothing beats hand written addresses so if possible, use it.

How to decide how often to write to your customers

Only your budget will decide how often you're going to write to your customers. But just sending them one letter is not really enough. Think of this as a long-term campaign to build your business. Of course you want to get good measurable results from your direct mail, but you're also building a relationship with your customers. So it is possible to write every week and not overdo it at all. In fact, a very successful idea is to create a campaign of three or four different letters emphasising different aspects of your business (service, prices, uniqueness, quality, etc.) to the same people spread over two to three weeks.

How to get the most from your post

Your local post office is a mine of useful information and a visit with the postmaster even before you've created your mailing piece would be time well spent.

What's the best way to send your mailing? If your letters are going to a fairly small area would second class be as effective as first? How many letters would you have to mail to get a discount?

Your post office is there to serve you and the postmaster will always be more than happy to talk with you about what you're trying to achieve. One particularly important service they can offer is to weigh your mailing piece and make sure it's within the basic cost limit. The last thing you need is to work hard to create a brilliant mailing piece, print it and stuff all your envelopes only to find that you're slightly over the weight and have to pay extra postage on every letter.

Direct mail is a very effective way to boost your business. You can get more customers, get your customers to spend more and even get them to make use of your business more regularly. The secret is to have a clear idea of what you want to achieve and then go for it. And when you've got the final draft that says exactly what you want it to say with all the "i"s dotted and "t"s crossed, read it out loud and be honest enough to say whether or not you'd buy what you're offering. If not, then start all over again. If yes, then you're ready to print and stuff your envelopes because you've designed a Winning Direct Mail Campaign.

TEN POINTS TO REMEMBER

1. The smaller your business the more cost effective direct mail is going to be for you.

2. The success of your direct mail campaign depends on three things:

   - The quality of your mailing list

   - The desirability of your product or service

   - The irresistibility of your offer.

3. The best mailing list is the one you create yourself either from your own customer list or from a list of potential customers who meet your specific criteria.

4. It's OK to hand-deliver your letters to save some money as long as it makes sense timewise.

5. Your direct mail letter is made up of five equally important constituent parts, each one of which fulfils a particular goal and builds to create an overall positive reaction from the reader:

   - The headline

- The body of the letter
- The PS
- The Inclusion
- The envelope

6. Use your customers to bring you more customers. Find a vehicle that allows them to invite their friends to spend money in your business and your campaign will be twice as successful as you'd hoped!

7. Don't be scared to use clichés in your advertising if it works. People respond to particular words and ideas and you should capitalise on those.

8. Nobody will buy anything from you unless there is a benefit to them. Your direct mail piece must answer the WII-FM question: **What's In It For Me?**

9. Keep your letter, message, envelope and use of fonts clear, concise and simple.

10. Make sure your mailing piece does not exceed the maximum weight for postage.

Example envelope:

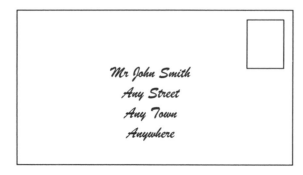

5

HOW TO WRITE ADS THAT WILL HIT THEIR "HOT BUTTONS"

How to beat the competition for your customers' attention

Around 75 per cent of all money spent on advertising by small business is spent on newspaper advertising. So let's try an experiment. Get a copy of a newspaper, look over the front page and then set it aside.

Now, what do you remember? Most people say, "Well there was something about . . . ", or "There was a picture of . . .".

When your customers are looking through the paper they give each page 3–4 seconds of their time. That's how long a story or ad has to get their attention, to get them to stop and pay attention to what it's all about.

That's why headlines and illustrations are so important. Because, just like letters, we read ads in a certain way and our brain processes the information as we go deciding whether or not we should continue spending time on this particular ad.

First we acknowledge the headline. If that seems relatively interesting, then we have a look at the illustration and if we're still interested, we take a look at the first paragraph of the story or ad and then decide if we want to know more and settle down to read the rest.

If you keep that in mind, you might just create an ad that works wonders!

- Headline

- Illustration

- First paragraph

- The rest.

And here's another fact that'll help you beat the competition for your customers' attention: only around 50 per cent of all printed ads actually ask you to buy their product. The rest of the ads look good, say nice things and might even win awards for creativity, but they don't actually ask for your business.

Now as far as I'm concerned, the whole point of spending time and money on advertising is to get the cash register ringing louder and more often. So if I'm writing an ad then I'm going to give the reader good reasons to buy my product or service, and then I'm going to ask them to step right up and show me the colour of their money! I'm going to make a promise, an offer, or a proposition that'll get them buying from me rather than from some other guy. That's why I advertise, and I assume you have the same goal in mind.

Your ad isn't going to hang on somebody's wall to be admired for its artistic or creative quality. It's an announcement, a call to action. You're telling people:

- "We're open for business — come and see us!"

- "We've slashed our prices — come and buy from us!"

- "Here's our new service — come and use it!"

- "We're the best there is — come and see why our prices are so high!"

Why you need to do your homework

I hate research. I hate taking time to read all about a new client's product, shop or service and ask questions about what they're trying to achieve and what makes them different to other people doing the same. And I particularly hate asking my client's customers what they think my client's strengths and weaknesses are.

But if I don't do this homework, if I haven't the slightest idea what makes my client different to others and if I don't know what my client's customers want, how can I begin to create ads that are relevant? More importantly, how can I know what aspects of my client's business appeal to his customers and potential customers enough to get them back into the shop or onto the phone?

I'm afraid the same can be said to you. If you haven't done your market research then don't do the advertising! You might be lucky, but chances are you'll be throwing your money into the wind. Taking time to do market research might seem like standing still, but it's always, always, worth the work: no pain, no gain.

Image, position and USP

Ad people love to use great sounding words and phrases to bamboozle clients and make it seem like they're doing something absolutely unique for which they have every right to charge vast sums of money — whether the ad works or not!

And let's be fair, a lot of companies have made fortunes because some ad man came up with a brilliant idea. "Coke: the real thing", "Avis — we try harder", "Guinness is good for you", and so on and so on. Many snappy phrases or images have made their way into our everyday psyche and even our language. Few of us vacuum, we "Hoover". Business people don't photocopy papers, they "Xerox" them.

So ad people aren't all bad and many of them deserve our respect. But for us in small business, it's very difficult to justify paying what most ad agencies charge and with a little time and thought we can probably do a pretty good job ourselves.

Fortunately, ad men love to talk about what they do and explain it to others, so now their secrets ain't so secret anymore!

Image

Exactly what image do you try to project about your company? If you have a restaurant do you put white linen tablecloths on the tables and dress your waiting staff in bow tie and tails? Or do you have bright but spartan decor and a self-service restaurant with the staff dressed in baseball hats and T-shirts? In both cases you're selling one product: food. But the "image" you're portraying to the public is poles apart and different people will respond to that image in particular ways.

Or if you're working from home, do you have a professional answering service pick up your calls when you're away, or does your partner answer in the kitchen with the children shouting and the washing machine on? Whichever "image" you portray will quickly be picked up on and reacted to by your customers.

So it is very important that whatever "image" you want to portray is reflected in your ad. The minds of readers are jolted if a seconds kitchen shop starts advertising that it now stocks fine china, or a wedding photographer also offers his services as a plasterer.

Not only will they be jolted, they'll also be confused and will stop being a customer of that particular business which will have lost all credibility.

Decide how you want to be perceived and create your advertising to enhance that image.

Position

Positioning of products or services was first analysed in the 1970s and has become a fairly important consideration for the advertising business. But it refers not so much to your service or product itself, but to how you are "positioned" in the mind of your customer.

It's important to you because it works on the principle that we all live in an over-communicated society. We're bombarded with advertising morning, noon and night on the radio and television, in our newspapers, on the backs of buses. Every time you turn around you are being asked to buy this or that. So your message must slice right through all of that and get into the psyche of your customers.

So positioning starts with the "product" — the merchandise, service, company, institution or even a person — but it's not what you do to the product, but rather what you do to the mind of your customer. You actually "position" your product in the mind of your customer.

Imagine a ladder in your mind. As the mind can only really cope with a maximum of a list of seven things (the 7 wonders of the world, the 7 deadly sins, the 7 dwarfs), this ladder only has 7 rungs on it. Each ladder refers to a product or service and how our mind "positions" each. There's quite a bit to the concept, but an easy example will show the basics.

Let's take fast food. If I say to you, "How about a quick bite to eat on the way to the pictures tonight?", your mind will bring its "fast food ladder" into focus and you'll run down the list from top to bottom in order of importance to you: McDonalds, Burger King, Kentucky Fried Chicken, the fish and chip shop, the pizza takeaway, the Chinese, the Indian.

That's the list our prospect has in his or her head. Your job, if you happen to own any of these, is to position your restaurant as far up the ladder as possible. If you're the fish and chip shop, then you must position yours to take that rung so that the customer doesn't simply think "fish and chip shop", but "Bob's fish and chip shop". By offering something unique to your business you will "position" it on the ladder of the mind of your customers and they will have no choice but to use you instead of somebody else.

USP

This brings us neatly to your USP: Unique Selling Proposition. What's special about your business that you can hang your hat on and say "this is me" and here's the image to back it up and the position I should command in people's minds?

What is it? Your market research will help identify it for you if you're not too sure yourself, but very often you will have started your business because you recognised a "hole in the market" which automatically gives you your USP.

Many of my clients tell me that they started their business because they saw an opportunity to do something nobody else was doing, or offer something nobody else was offering. But they forget to tell people what is special about their business and don't take full advantage of what they have.

Mary was 21 when I met her. She had always fancied being a photographer and had fiddled about with films and lenses since she was 12. After she left school at 18 she took a few courses in photography to get some theory to back up her practical knowledge and apprenticed herself to a wedding photographer. And her photos were nothing less than fantastic. Full of beauty, atmosphere and passion she showed herself able to do a great job.

Then she started on her own advertising herself as:

Mary White (FPPS) (MFWP)

Wedding Photographer

and business went fairly well. But not great, so she asked me to take some time to help her.

My first question was what do the initials stand for? They were Fellow of the Professional Photographers Society (FPPS), and Member of the Federation of Wedding Photographers (MFWP). In fact, Mary was the only photographer within 50 miles that had either, let alone both, of these qualifications. But she wasn't telling anybody about it. Until then.

Along with a few other minor changes, we started to advertise her qualifications to position her as the only real professional wedding photographer in her area.

"Nobody Else is Qualified to Take Your Wedding Photographs"

"Would You Let an Amateur Conduct Your Wedding Ceremony? Well Don't Let One Take Your Photographs Either!"

Now these were pretty strong headlines and I wasn't sure if Mary would go with them. But she had the guts to say yes and we very quickly established her credibility as the "professional" wedding photographer in her area. Others have now added the letters to their names, but she was the first and she has the top rung as far as the people in that area are concerned.

By using her Unique Selling Proposition — the thing that made her different — to her advantage, she was able to create an image and position that will never be removed from the ladder in her customers' minds.

Your USP is very often looking you right in the face so try not to miss it. Think about why you decided to start your business and marry it with your market research to find what makes you stand out from the crowd.

When Albert started Courtesy Cabs he had an idea that offering extra service would help build his business. His drivers would open doors, help with luggage or shopping, never smoke in the cab and always wear a shirt and tie. Nothing fancy, but just a little different.

He contacted me after having been in business for three years and asked for a little help to "drum up a bit of extra business". While we were chatting I asked him why he had chosen the name and he went through his list of little extras his drivers did.

"Great", I said. "And who have you told about this?"

Well of course he'd told his drivers, his wife and his mother. But that was about it. He hadn't actually mentioned it to the public. But then, you don't, do you?

Of course you do, and we did. We created an invitation. It was printed on stiff card about the size of a wedding invitation and put one through each of the 15,000 doors in his town.

On the other side of the card we listed telephone and fax numbers, times of opening and other general information. And in the version that went into the paper we changed the "Please keep this card" to "Please cut out and keep".

So we had achieved a lot with one simple mail drop/newspaper ad:

1. We had projected the image Albert wanted by projecting it on our invitation

2. We had positioned Albert as the most courteous cab company in the area

3. We had done it by simply advertising the USP: courtesy. After all, that's why Albert had started the business and it's what he wanted to offer, so why keep it to himself?

PLEASE KEEP THIS CARD

We would like your help.

At Courtesy Cabs we pride ourselves on our . . . well . . . courtesy. And we'd like you to tell us if we're living up to our name.

Next time you use our service I would really appreciate your giving us marks out of ten just to let us know that we're doing things properly.

So please keep this card and see if we really earn the name

Courtesy Cabs
01122-445566

Please score us out of 10:
- ❑ When you called, was the telephone answered promptly and courteously?
- ❑ Was the driver friendly and courteous?
- ❑ Was the Cab spotlessly clean and smelled fresh?
- ❑ Did the Driver open the door for you?
- ❑ Did the Driver help with your luggage or shopping?

There aren't any formulas to success in creating your ad. As you get more and more confident in your creativity you can begin to play around with them. But we've got to have a starting point to allow you to start writing your ads now, today, so here it is:

Your Headline Has Got to Make Them Stop in Their Tracks!

Your graphic has got to get them involved with your ad and be relevant to your headline

If they've got as far as your first paragraph you're doing well. Don't push your luck. Keep it simple and to the point.

Now they're really involved in your ad you can begin to go to town on the offer.

Here's where your logo
goes, not on top.

Snazzy "strap line". Tells the reader what you think of you.

There are endless ways to actually lay out your ad even just using this as the model. So do be adventurous as long as your ad always:

- Promotes your Unique Selling Proposition (USP)

- Projects an image that you want and can sustain

- Calls your reader to act: "come in . . ." — "send for . . ." — "order by . . ."

The headline

The same rules that applied to writing your direct mail letter apply with your newspaper ad: it's got to be read, it's got to excite, it's got to be believable and it's got to draw your reader into your ad. This is the red light, the sign that says "Hey you. Give me a minute of your time here. I've got something you want".

It doesn't have to be a free offer or an amazing discount to get people's attention, although there's no doubt that both of those certainly work. One of my clients went with the headline

"Here's Why We're the Most Expensive Men's Shop in Town"

You can bet that got a few eyes looking through the ad.

And three years ago I worked with a client who owns a bookshop to develop the "If you love . . ." ad which he's still using. He simply highlights a book each time he advertises. He uses his headline to bring interested people into his ad — and ultimately his shop.

If You Love Horses . . .

     . . . you'll love (picture of cover of horsey book)

Short description of the book along with price.

         Telephone number to reserve
         your copy from a limited stock

         Address of shop where to
         pick your book up (Logo)

It really couldn't be easier. See if this formula might work for your business and use it. It works! And it works because it's simple and makes the promise right there in the headline drawing the reader into the ad itself.

The illustration

Use of illustrations in your ad is a must. You might choose to use a photo or a drawing or a diagram, but use something that is relevant to and supports your headline. You'd be surprised just how many people — including the professional ad men — don't. For example, I just saw an ad last week for an international hotel company who were pushing their golf breaks, and their graphic was a line drawing of a pen! Did I miss something or is this slightly irrelevant? The result of this interesting juxtaposition was my trying to figure out what was going on and not actually reading what was undoubtedly a super ad.

Your illustration needs to be the second line in your assault on the mind and eyes of the reader. Along with the headline it needs to draw your reader into the ad. It needs to appeal. It needs to make a visual promise or an offer that is enough to make your readers want to find out more.

My suggestion would be to make your illustration as simple as possible. If you're selling office equipment, show office equipment. Don't be tempted to be so creative that your readers will have to think hard to make the connection, because they won't. In the 3 or 4 seconds that they spend on the page your ad is on they will simply ignore your terribly clever graphics and go on to the guy who sells nuts and bolts and shows nuts and bolts.

You shouldn't take your customers for fools, but neither should you assume that they will engage their intellect when giving your ad the once-over.

The body copy

You've worked hard to get them this far, don't lose them now!

Have a look at some of the copy in ads in your local paper or magazines. Some of it is atrocious. It becomes a list of features and things that the vendor thinks is important. It's not written for your consumption, it's written to make the managing director feel good about his brilliant company or product.

Often the problem is that the owner of the company — you — is so close to the day-to-day running of the thing that they can't actually stand back and see what they have to offer from the perspective of the customer. And very often it's the owner who insists on writing the copy for the ad. The result: verbosity. Here's an example of an ad I was asked to review and amend (I've changed a few details to save embarrassment):

> "Here at Mills Heating we are involved in on-going research and development of our full line of products. Therefore we are considered to be the leader in our field. Our name is recognised and respected throughout the country and is the first stop for consumers hoping to add a touch of excitement to their homes through the implementation of our innovative methods. We

can give you an estimate of the cost of putting
our system in your home anytime."

Well that's going to get you excited, isn't it? That's going to raise you from your chair right now and head off
in search of "implementing the innovative methods" in
your home.

I don't think so! The writer — actually the managing
director — was writing for himself, not for his customers. To be fair, he wasn't telling anything but the truth,
but he seemed to lack a certain flair. Or so I told him.
And to his credit, he agreed to let me rewrite the copy
of his ad for him. To address it to his end users. To
make a promise to his potential customers and get a
response.

> "When you're looking for the latest in heating
> technology, you're looking for Mills heating.
> Every boiler and radiator system in our exten-
> sive range has been extensively researched to
> make your home warm and energy efficient.
> After all, in an era when energy is so expensive
> you don't want to waste money on an inefficient
> system.
>
> We have showrooms around the country and
> would be thrilled to have an opportunity to
> show you how we slash the cost of heating your
> home. Please call for a free, no-obligation con-
> sultation, or visit a showroom nearest you."

So what has been changed? We've still told readers
we're the best company in home heating and we've
asked them to come and visit. Except in the original we
told how great we were, and in the new version we've

told them how our being so great can benefit them. And we've specifically asked them to get off their seats and come in to see us. We've offered a promise and we've asked for a response. Words are funny old things and how you use them to emphasise a point will make the difference between an ad that gets people responding or get them yawning.

The tag or strap line

All this jargon! Well, a "strap line" is the one-liner that sets the tone for your company. Some well-known ones are "Avis. We're number 2 so we try harder." "Ronseal. It does exactly what it says on the tin." "Miller Beer. The taste of America."

All of these lines work toward positioning, image and USP. They encapsulate what the company thinks about itself. Most importantly, they're effective.

Not every ad has a tag-line and, to be honest, many that do shouldn't have bothered! An advert I've seen recently — not one of my clients, I hasten to add — has the strap line, "Showing the competition a clean pair of heels". Now what's this for? A sports shoe company, perhaps? Or even a shoe polish company? No. It's for a double-glazing company. Maybe it works for them, but I don't see what it does for their position, image, or USP. In fact, I don't think it's relevant to them at all. But somebody probably charged them a small fortune to come up with it and so they have it splashed all over their vans.

So if you're going to have a tag-line, make sure it's relevant to your company, your product or your service. Otherwise, don't waste your time trying to come up with something wonderful. Ask yourself, if I didn't know what company this is for, could I guess just from the tag-line. If the answer is no, then think seriously about using it.

How to make money from classified ads

Don't tell the advertising manager at your local paper that I told you, but it is actually quite possible to get a better return on your investment from a classified ad than from its more expensive cousin, the display. It doesn't always work, and I'm certainly not suggesting you throw all your display ads in the bin. But there are times when using the classified columns can be very profitable.

You need only take a look at the ads in papers such as *Exchange and Mart* to know that there is a place for the classified ads.

A client of mine owns a lumber yard. He sells just about every size and shape of lumber you could ask for and even has a range of finished products such as garden fences, pergolas, garden seats and — if you can believe it — flagpoles (somebody has to sell them)!

For a long time he had been spending a lot of money on display ads trying to think of different ways to promote his business with clever headlines and smart copy, but he knew he was only ever getting a small percentage of his stock mentioned and didn't feel he was presenting his business properly.

When we got together and had a bit of a chat we decided that what he really wanted to make a point of was that (1) he had the best selection of lumber available in the area, and (2) that he was as competitively priced as anybody else. We also knew that he had two markets: the local builders and the local DIY'ers.

So we decided to change tack completely. First we developed a fairly inexpensive brochure which listed all of the different types and sizes of wood he had available. Then we developed a mailing list of local builders and sent them the brochure with a covering letter guaranteeing that he would match or beat any price they got for lumber anywhere in the area. We also said that this brochure would be updated monthly, and added a couple of "specials" each month depending on what he felt the demand would be at that time.

Reaching the DIY'ers was a bit more of a challenge and we looked at the advertising possibilities. The local paper had a good circulation and by asking quite a few readers about the paper we discovered that they all read the "For Sale" column. One man said, "Even if I'm not looking for anything in particular I always find something of interest in that column".

So we decided to advertise in the classified "For Sale" column with a simple list of available lumber and prices. Every ad ended with: "And this is just a sample of what we have to offer. Call (0123) 446789". In addition, we decided to take another ad in the same column specifically for garden products during the summer months.

The results: sales of lumber to builders grew substantially because of the direct mail campaign. Sales of lumber to DIY'ers stayed about the same. And sales of garden products rose by 20 per cent. Nothing spectacular, it's true. But advertising costs were slashed by an amazing 70 per cent which amounted to almost £3,000 per year.

That's certainly one use of the classified ad. But it is also an excellent vehicle for businesses trying to develop a mailing list. In fact, that's exactly what an alternative medicine client of mine used with great success, and it could be used by any business which sold either an easily posted product or provided a service that didn't require a personal visit.

Alexandra had qualified as an aromatherapist and set up a small practice in a market town of about 25,000. She advertised in the local paper and began to get a fairly steady flow of clients who loved the massages and oils. In fact, many of them bought the oils for their own use at home between visits.

Business was good but not great and Alex was stuck for ideas to expand. No matter how much advertising she did she seemed to have tapped out the market. One new customer seemed to simply replace one that decided to stop coming.

We met for lunch and discussed the idea of expanding her business into other areas by developing a mail order clientele for her oils and booklets on aromatherapy. Initially she balked at the idea saying that she didn't really want to be a retailer, she wanted to be an aromatherapist working with individuals on a one-to-one personal basis.

So we chatted some more and I pointed out that really she would have to move to a bigger town or city to build her business that way. But I did acknowledge her preferences and suggested that she could offer a free telephone consultation with every purchase of say £10 or more of product. (To be honest, I thought this was a bit ridiculous at the time but I was to be proved wrong.)

We placed several classified ads in papers within a 50-mile radius. In the ads we encouraged people simply to send/phone for a free catalogue — "free" being the magic word with ads like this. No commitment needed and you get something for free as well. In return all you have to provide is your name and address. Simple!

Here's the ad we used:

FEEL GREAT all over with European aromatherapy oils. FREE catalogue of oils and advice. Call Alex (0123) 456789.

The response was terrific and I was absolutely amazed at the numbers of catalogues that went out the door in the first week — no less than 107! And with every catalogue went a short letter of introduction promising FREE telephone consultation (their call) with any £10 worth of product purchased. In other words, if you agreed to purchase £10 worth of goods, Alex would spend some time on the phone with you going over what you were looking for from aromatherapy and suggest specific products for you.

A few minutes on the phone and a credit card number later and you were a customer for life. It was an incredible success. I was forced to admit that her free consultation idea was a winner, and she agreed that it was the best £5.30 she had ever spent — and continues to spend each week!

How to write classified ads that get results

By definition writing a classified ad is a very different proposition to creating a display ad. It's not necessarily easier but there are certainly different elements which are important.

In many ways writing a good classified ad demands a higher level of discipline than the display ad. You have less room to work with, you have no illustrations and you have to get your message over without the help of a headline.

Your best bet is to start by looking at other ads that are similar to the one you will hope to place. See how they are constructed and decide whether or not they are good, i.e. would you respond to that ad.

You'll find that the first few words of the ad are the most important. They are the ones in capital letters and really act as your headline as they catch the eye first. Do not start your ad FOR SALE! You might laugh, but look at how many people do it. Obviously if it's in the FOR SALE column it will be for sale!

Your first few words should include a good emotive word or two. "Free" is always a good one. So are "feel great"; "be healthy"; "make money" "save money", in fact anything that will make the eye stop and look through the rest of the ad.

Make your offer quickly. This is a classified ad and people reading it will not scan line after line of copy. Keep it to four lines if you can (about 20–25 words) including the telephone number. There is something psychological about reading a long classified ad that says to the mind "this one is too long, don't read it", and you simply skip to the next.

Make it as easy as possible to get the information you're offering. If you're offering a catalogue or brochure (and I would strongly suggest that this is the route you take if using classified ads), then make them simple to get. What you actually want to happen is to have the person reading the ad fold the paper and call you immediately.

To do that you have to offer a telephone number. There is no point in asking them to write for information because they won't. They'll want to. They might even tear your ad out to write later. But they won't get around to doing it . . . ever!

But give people a telephone number to call to get free information, and you'll get a great response. Make it a toll-free number and you'll get an even better result, but I wouldn't suggest you make that investment just yet!

Make sure you will have the telephone answered, if not by you then by somebody who knows what is going on, or an answering machine with a message specifically dedicated to this arrangement. People will not call a second time. You must make arrangements to have their call taken by somebody — or something — that will let them leave a name and address and a phone number if possible.

Every time you make it more difficult to get to you, you lessen your chances of making a sale. If people have to write instead of call they'll think twice. If they don't get an answer the first time they call, they'll think twice about calling the second time, etc., etc. Your classified ad strategy is a five step process:

1. Give away some free information that people will want.

2. Make it easy to get that information by simply picking up the telephone and leaving their name and address.

3. Get the free information to them ASAP along with an opportunity to spend money on your product.

4. Get their names onto your mailing list.

5. Write to them regularly with "offers", "specials" and "seasonal sales".

Finally, find some way to monitor your ads. If you are placing ads in more than one paper then add something to each that will differentiate them from each other. The best would be different telephone numbers to call, but that is impractical unless you want to get into mail order in a big way.

The most sensible is to make the offer slightly different each time. Newspaper A might have an ad that reads " . . . call for your free brochure"; paper B's might read " . . . call for your free catalogue"; and paper C's could say " . . . call for your free information". It seems a small thing, but unless you are actually taking each call and able to ask where did you see our ad, you need to have a way to distinguish the source. People leaving a message on your answering machine will use the terms you used in your ad.

Once you have run the ad for a few weeks you can begin to see exactly where the best results are coming from and might decide to drop certain papers and take others on.

How to write an advertorial

Sooner or later you will have the opportunity to be involved with an "advertorial". Basically, this is something that will appear in the paper or magazine as an editorial, but you will have had every opportunity to control its content — and will have paid for the privilege.

Common advertorials are the ones written around "Things to See and Do in . . ." or "Places to Stay in . . ." in local or regional papers. The newspaper or magazine will approach a certain number of suppliers in your particular business/industry sector and will give you the opportunity to buy an ad. In return you will get the added incentive of having your ad set around a nice editorial piece in the middle which will talk-up your business and sound totally unbiased.

Somewhere on the page it will also say "advertorial feature" or some such term to cover the paper from being accused of bias.

The benefits of an advertorial are mixed. You will have control of the content of the piece about your business, but you must also accept that there will be many of your competitors appearing in the same piece, thus diluting your message.

It is, of course, quite possible and feasible for you to create your own advertorial and pay for the space in the paper. You could write a very nice piece about yourself in relatively unbiased but glowing terms. It would be written in a journalistic style and you would then go along to your local paper with ad and photos in one hand and cheque in the other.

Alternatively, you could organise a few of your fellow, non-competitive business friends to come in with you and develop the same idea but splitting the cost. Obviously, every additional name will take away from the impact of your own piece, but that would be the trade-off for dividing the cost with others.

If you decide to go with the advertorial as planned and organised by your local paper/magazine, then get in touch with the advertising manager of the publication and ask for a copy of their advertorial schedule. If they don't have one you should suggest they get one quickly, and then ask if maybe this person is in the wrong job!

If you find that they have one that is suitable for you, why not suggest that *you* write the editorial. After all, you're the one who is knowledgeable in the field and you would be able to do it easily. There are a number of benefits to this: (1) you'll have an amount of control over the content, (2) you'll add to your label of "expert" in the field, and (3) given that you will be acknowledged as the author, you'll have an added mention in the piece.

If they don't go for you writing the editorial itself, maybe you can help them in some other way. Would they like some background information? A graph, maybe? Or a photo? Either way, take the opportunity to get involved in the event and prove yourself indispensable to the running of the paper!

Radio and TV advertorials

Not quite as popular in the electronic media, I suppose you could say that when an author is interviewed he or she is taking the time to do an advertorial when they tell you the name of the book, the cost and who published it! But there aren't really that many chances for the average business to benefit from such an opportunity.

But watch out for every opportunity you have to get in there and promote your business.

TEN POINTS TO REMEMBER

1. Your ad has about 3 seconds to get the attention of a newspaper reader. The headline is the most important eye-catcher in your ad.

2. In order of importance, your ad will have four pieces:

    *   Headline

    *   Illustration

    *   First paragraph of copy

    *   The rest of the ad.

3. You shouldn't even think of creating an ad until you've carried out at least the very minimum amount of market research.

4. Hit them early with your USP: Unique Selling Proposition.

5. Use your ads to position your business on their "mind ladder".

6. Don't be scared to be aggressive in your ad. Ask for their business!

7. Use the formula in the example until you feel confident enough to create your own ideas.

8. Consider the possibility of using the classified columns either as your primary advertising, or as support to your display ads.

9. Use classified ads as a means of developing a mailing list rather than as an end in themselves: the two-step sale.

10. Monitor the success of your ads by asking everybody where they heard about your business and be prepared to pull ads or extend their lives according to their effectiveness.

6

HOW TO CREATE RADIO ADS THAT WILL GET RESULTS

And a few words about TV

How to decide whether or not to advertise on radio

I love radio. I love to listen to it and I love to write for it. But I always ask my clients to be wary of adding it to their budget. It can be expensive and unless you're absolutely sure of your market, it can be irrelevant as you send your message out over the ether to deaf ears.

So how can you decide if radio advertising is a good investment for you and your business? Like every other form of advertising, unfortunately, it contains an in-built element of hit and miss. However, there are a few questions you should ask yourself at the outset which will help get the odds in your favour. If you can't agree with all of them you should be asking yourself if you can afford to spend money that might be better spent elsewhere. If you can't agree with most of them, then you need to go back to your market research and see if your ads are going to get to your target market. And if you can't agree with any of them, forget it. Radio is not for you!

- It is legal and ethical for me to advertise my service/product.

- I can clearly identify a time when my target market will be listening to the radio (business programme, news programme, travel programme, other specialised programmes).

- I can write my own ad or can afford to have my ad written for me.

- I can afford to put a lengthy campaign in place which will get my ad aired a number of times per day/week.

- My radio station agrees to let me be involved with every step of the process.

- My radio station can sell me a package that makes financial sense and allows me to advertise at times when I know my target audience is going to be listening.

For your radio advertising to be effective it doesn't matter so much about how brilliant the content is, but rather that you are getting the message out at a time when your target audience is going to receive it. If you can't guarantee that then it's not worth the money you're spending.

And you'll probably spend a lot. Unlike print ads, radio ads come and go in 30 seconds. There's no way of setting them aside to look at later or pass them on to somebody else. You've got 30 seconds to get your message across effectively and get a positive reaction.

Actually, you can buy radio time in 10 second increments (10, 20, 30, 40, 50 and 60 second ads), and while the 30 second slot is considered to be the standard for small businesses, you can choose what is right for you. And yes, it is possible to get a simple message across in only 10 seconds, but it has to be every simple and easily understood. How about arranging to have a 10 second ad read after every news bulletin? So, for example, instead of having 3 x 30 second ads a day you might have 9 x 10 second ads.

If your message is simple and clear, people will get to know that it's coming up after/before/during the news/traffic report/weather, and will be ready to receive it. It's unusual, but if you want to make an impact and your station is willing to work with you, why not? For example, if you're a car tyre dealer why not get your ad in after the traffic news. Something simple like:

> "Don't let your tyres let you down. Get a free tread check at Harry's Tyres. Main Street, Your town."

I can't think of a more simple message put out over the airways when motorists — the target market — are going to be listening.

Or how about a quick ad after the time-check?

> "It's 3 O'clock. Still time to pick up a pizza from Bob's Pizzeria. Call 555-1212."

The point is, your ad doesn't have to conform to any particular format and can be as simple as you like. A lot has to do with the willingness of your particular local radio station to work with you to give you what you want. Use your imagination and a little friendly persuasion. It can work miracles!

How to get your timing just right

One of the challenges with writing scripts for radio is the need to fill a certain length of time. This is something of an art, but anybody can master it with a bit of effort. Radio stations are funny places. If you've bought a 20 second slot then they want your ad to last 20 seconds. Not 19 seconds or 21 seconds, but 20 on the nose. So when you're writing your ad it needs to be exactly 20 seconds long.

So here's the challenge: how many words can you put into 20 seconds? Well if you're like me and you talk too fast for anybody to understand a word you're saying, you could well decide that you can put 75 words into 20 seconds. But nobody would actually hear your message. So what you need is a clock with a second hand beside you and the determination to read your ad out loud (regardless of the fact that the neighbours are going to think you've taken leave of your senses as you repeat things to yourself) and time everything carefully. You'll need to speak quite slowly and watch the clock until you have the right number of words for the time allotted.

If you do find it too difficult, write out what you want and let the folks at the radio station tweak it a little to get it into the time slot and ready to go. As long as you can give them the gist of what you want to say and an idea of the important points, they should be able to put something together for you. But do try it yourself first. It's great fun using your imagination to promote your business and incredibly satisfying when it works and people start congratulating you on your wizardry with the spoken word!

How to be absolutely positive your money is being well spent

This is just a word of warning if you do decide to do some radio advertising (and I hope you will if you're confident that it's relevant because it's great fun). You must be sure to keep control of the process at all times. There will be a temptation to let yourself be guided by the "experts" at the station, and that's fine — to a point. But do not allow them to take over your advert. After all, it's your product, it's your business and it's your money. Therefore, you have every right to be a part of the process from the creation of the ad through the studio mixing of the ad to the times you want the ad to be aired. If your station does not allow you to be a part of any or all of those stages then stop the process immediately.

In other words, keep control at all times. And the most important thing as I have already mentioned — but which bears repeating — is to be absolutely sure of the slots/times you are buying. Do not be tempted to buy a cheap package that gives the radio station control of the time your ad gets aired. In the short term you'll save money on the package, but your results will suffer as your ads will hit the airwaves at times when nobody you want to hear then is even awake, let alone ready to make a buying decision.

How to add structure to your ads

So now you've decided to write your own ad. You get out the pen and paper and stare at the white emptiness of the whole thing. After 15 painful minutes of doodling and squirming you tear up the paper, snap the pencil in half and tell yourself and your partner that you're just not a script-writer.

And maybe you're not. But you've only got to turn on the radio and listen to a few commercials for a minute or two to soon realise that the ideas you have are just as good as and possibly even better than the ones the so-called professionals have. So instead of giving up, start by giving the script some structure and then filling in the details later.

The beauty of radio ads is that you can develop whatever scenario your mind can think of. If you want to have your ad sound like it's coming from a mountain top, the bottom of the ocean or the inside of a dungeon, it can be done. There really isn't any limitation to your creativity but I would caution against being too outlandish. While you can be exciting, innovative and fresh in your approach, you should also try to make your location relevant to your ad.

For example, when a client asked me to write an ad to push their new frozen food selection I wrote it as an interview with an Eskimo. Now that was a little different, but it worked because it was relevant to the product and message. So be creative, but don't strain credulity.

Once you have thought of an idea you've only got 30 seconds to make an impact. Therefore your ad must achieve two things very quickly:

1.   The listeners must know *who* is advertising, and

2.   They have to know *what* you are advertising.

Sound simple? Well it is. But listen to those radio ads again and see how long it is before you even know who's advertising let alone what they're advertising. For reasons that make no sense, script-writers try to be too clever, get involved in some smart story line and forget what their job is: sell the product.

Don't make the same mistake.

1. Tell them who you are in the first line, and then tell them as often as possible

2. Tell them what you have to offer in the second line, and tell them often.

And because you're working with such a short time span you've got to get them to hear your ad. So set out in the first place to get their attention and don't worry if somebody tells you it's not sophisticated. It doesn't have to be fancy, it just has to work. So how about starting with "excuse me!" in a loud voice or "stop that immediately!". Will this approach win you prizes at the next ad award dinner? No. Will it get a couple more listeners to pay attention, hear your ad, buy your product and put a few more pounds on the bottom line? Could be. So do it.

Seven successful methods for writing scripts that work

So now you've decided to tell them who you are and what you're offering. You've thought up a brilliant scenario and you've made a few notes on what you'd like to say. Now how do you put some meat on those bones?

There are a number of different methods that copy-writers use to create an ad that will work for their clients. There aren't that many different approaches available so these are often just variations on a theme. In order to keep everything easily understood you can really only have two voices being used in your ad. There are two reasons for this: (1) you're writing an ad, not a soap opera — any more than two voices will confuse listeners who aren't keen on listening to ads in the first place, and (2) it would be prohibitively expensive to have more than two voices. So your choices are the same as the pros:

1.   Single voice over

2.   Dialogue — two voices

3.   Dramatisation where you've set scenes and locations

4.   A combination of 1 and 3.

That's it. There are no other possibilities. However, it's what you do with those possibilities that can make your ad interesting or boring, successful or a failure. So you need to have access to the 7 successful ways to approach your script, and here they are. I would recommend you use number 7 at the early stage of your script writing career. But do get more ambitious as time goes on. Be careful that your script is neither ridiculous nor incredible and keep your ideas simple and easy to understand.

1. Slice of life

This is a very popular script writing technique. A couple of people meet and discuss your product/service. One is trying to convince the other to use yours and finally succeeds without sounding ridiculous. Here's one approach that is a bit over the top:

> *Lady 1*: "I see you're using new improved Sinkex."
>
> *Lady 2*: "Oh yes. New Sinkex with the all powerful detergents and bleach keeps my sink sparkling clean. In fact, my children love to look at themselves in the shining sink."
>
> *Lady 1*: "Great! I'll just dash down to the shop and buy a bottle for my sink."

Realistic? I don't think so. Certainly, I've never heard anybody talking quite like that. But with a few changes in wording and emphasis it can be made to sound a lot more feasible.

> *Lady 1*: "Mary, I'm whacked. I've been scrubbing that sink all morning and I still can't get the stains to shift."
>
> *Lady 2*: "Relax Jane. I have the answer. I've been using new Sinkex and it's great. Not only does it shift the stains, but it has some new bleach that kills the germs as well. And you won't strain your arm scrubbing."

A bit more realistic. Sure it's still unusual for two women to have a major discussion about their dirty sink, but this presentation is a bit more credible than the original. The best way for you to check your own script is to write your dialogue and then say it out loud to yourself. If it sounds corny to you then you can bet your life it's going to sound ridiculous to your listeners. But if it sounds OK to you then they'll probably go along with it as well.

2. Give them the answer

This is a follow-on to the "slice of life" theme but doesn't necessarily require dialogue. It's a play on the "feature and benefit" approach we took earlier. You outline a problem your customer will recognise, and then tell them how you can solve the problem for them.

> *Announcer*: "When you want to pick up a few groceries and get home quickly you don't want to be standing behind cart loads of food and screaming kids. That's why at Fred's Market we have introduced the 'Quick Shop' lanes. If you have ten items or less, we can get you headed home again faster than you would believe."

You've outlined a problem that your market research has shown up and solved it for your customers. It's a simple but effective method of advertising.

3. Have your customers tell it like it is

Testimonials are always effective in ads when a third party assures your customers that they've tried your product or service and it works or meets their needs. In the big leagues businesses often use celebrities to promote their wares and that can be met with mixed success. But unless you're happy to fork out thousands of pounds to have some celebrity tell your story, stick with something more sensible. The beauty about testimonials using ordinary everyday customers is that the less polished they are, the better and more realistic they will appear to be. And better still, you probably won't even need to write a script!

However, you will need to find a professional interviewer with access to the necessary recording equipment. Ask your station for help and advice on this and be sure your interviewer has a list of questions to ask that are relevant to your business and will encourage your customers to say the right things. Once you've done the recordings you can get the best bits spliced together by the station to create an effective ad.

4. Being the voice of your own business

Some business people love to ham it up and be their own promoter. Sometimes it works, and sometimes it doesn't. If you're thinking about being the voice of your own business and telling your own story then you've got to be honest enough with yourself to know whether or not that is a good idea.

Do you have a strong accent or a flat voice? If so, then it might not be a good idea. Are you well known in the area? If so, then your voice might be recognised and the ad will work fine. Can you talk without actually sounding like you're reading a script? If you can then go ahead. But if not, don't — under any circumstances — be tempted down this road as you will sound terrible and your ad will suffer.

Be honest with yourself. Ask trusted friends and family to critique your efforts and live by their decision. Remember that the few pounds saved by being your own announcer will fade into insignificance if your own voice is too weak to carry the message or you sound like the amateur you are.

5. Newsy

This is one of those "have you heard" ads. Have you heard about the new shop? Have you heard about our new opening hours? Have you heard about our new product range? They're a successful type of ad and work well for old and new businesses alike. So if you are always coming up with new ideas for your business and they stand advertising, then this is a good method to use. Make it newsworthy and then write an ad that promotes it. And it really doesn't matter what it is. For example, one of my clients changed the label on their packs of cheese and wanted to get this "exciting" information to their customers. I decided this would stand a "newsy" approach and came up with this:

> *Announcer*: (Gradually getting more excited.) "I've got to tell you something really exciting about Ashland cheese. It's the country's favourites cheese. You know that. And of course you know that Ashland Cheese is made with only the purest milk.
>
> But now every cheese from Ashland has a new label! It's bright . . . it's informative . . . it's . . . it's . . . brilliant. Trust Ashland Cheese to create a brilliant label for a brilliant taste. It's brilliant, I tell you, brilliant. (Realising he's a little bit over the top.) Anyway, I just wanted to tell you."
>
> *Second announcer*: "Ashland Cheese. It tastes so great that you'll want to tell everybody."

So here's proof positive that even the exciting news that a label has been changed can be made into an effective radio ad.

6. Using humour

Here's dangerous ground if ever there was! I love humorous ads and I can even remember the punchline of most of the jokes I tell. But I'm not very good at writing humorous material. Actually very few people are, although a lot try. So you need to be careful with the use of humour in ads.

But, if you are able to write something that will make people smile or laugh you can be sure they'll remember your product or service fondly. More importantly, if things don't work out in your chosen business, you might well have a career in advertising!

Use humour very, very carefully. It can backfire on you if what you think is side-splittingly funny comes across as ridiculous or even daft to your customers. If you do use humour, remember that the goal is to have them laughing *with* you, not *at* you.

Here's one idea I had for the Ashland's Cheese people that they felt was humorous and might even get a smile from their customers. See what you think!

> (In a supermarket.)
>
> Lady 1: (Loud voice) "Excuse me!"
>
> *Lady 2:* "Me?"
>
> *Lady 1:* "I love the great taste of Ashland Cheese, you know."
>
> *Lady 2:* "Pardon?"
>
> *Lady 1:* "Oh yes. Ashland Cheese tastes great. (Conspiratorially) Do you know my husband?"
>
> *Lady 2:* "I don't even know you."
>
> *Lady 1:* "Well, my husband would leave me if I didn't buy Ashland Cheese."

Lady 2: "Listen. I'm sorry. I don't know you. I don't know your husband, I've already bought my Ashland Cheese and I really am in a hurry."

Lady 1: "Of course dear, of course. Still, it's great that we've had this chance for a chat."

Announcer: "Ashland Cheese. It tastes so great you've got to tell everybody."

7. Talking heads (the one I recommend you start with)

This is the rather uncomplimentary name for ads that have one person simply telling you how great a product or service is. There are two great things about this type of ad: (1) They're easy for the first-time scriptwriter to write, and (2) they work. Ad men hate them, but they are one of the most effective methods of getting your message across simply.

And these sort of ads can be as basic or creative as you want them to be. Radio stations can create atmosphere, background music or noises and a sense of "place" for just about anything using sophisticated special effects. So if you want your announcer to be in a busy street or the quiet front room of his or her house, your station can do it for you. All you need to do is give them the words and the idea and they will "mix" it all together to create a very effective final result.

For example, I was asked to write an ad for a liquor store. That morning I had heard that the actor Robert Mitchum had died and decided to write the ad in an American private detective/1940s style. A sort of recognition for the pleasure his movies had always given me.

To create the atmosphere I put my private detective in a car with the windshield wipers going. It would be raining heavily.

> *SFX*: (notification used to let the engineer know of the need for special effects) We're in a car. It's raining. The wipers are going.
>
> *Announcer*: (Mitchum-type voice): "It had been a tough day and I just wanted to slip off my shoes and enjoy a quiet drink. But where was the nearest liquor store? I let my mind wander over the choices. Then it hit me like a 40 tonne truck. Mahoneys. They're always open, and they've got the best prices around. As I pulled up in front of Mahoneys a redhead with eyes you could swim in and legs that went on forever caught my arm. But that's a story for another day."
>
> *Announcer 2*: "Mahoneys. We're open when you need us and we guarantee the best prices in town. Redheads are optional."

The studio that mixed this ad really went to town and you felt you were right in the car with the character with the rain bouncing off the roof. In fact they went a step further and had the car door open and close when the character arrived in front of Mahoneys. So nothing is impossible if you just use your imagination.

That's fairly creative, but you might simply want your announcer to give the details of your offer simply and without any razzmatazz, and that can be equally as effective. For example, here's a script I did for a client who was opening a new car showroom. He didn't want any fanfare or anything that suggested that he was a typical "second-hand car dealer". He simply wanted a message that said:

- He had been in business for some time

- He was opening a new showroom in town

- He was opening on Saturday, February 10th, at 10:00 a.m.

- Every visitor on opening day could enter a draw for a holiday in Florida.

So I put a few thoughts on paper and talked to him about being his own promoter — to make the ad using his voice. He agreed:

> (Loud Voice) "Hello!
>
> I'm Ted Waters and I own Waters Motors. If you don't know me, maybe you'll remember my dad, John. He started our business back in 1952 and our family has been serving yours ever since.
>
> Now we're opening a new car showroom in Templo and I'd love to show you all the exciting 1997 models we have in stock. I also think you'll find something very attractive about the super financing package we've put together for our first 100 customers.
>
> But even if you don't want to buy a new car just yet, I'd like to meet you. So why not bring the family down to the new Waters Motors Show-room on our opening day, Saturday, February 10th. We'll have balloons and other goodies for the kids, and you can enter our prize draw to take the whole family on a fantastic holiday to Florida."

> *Announcer*: "Waters Motors. Opening in Templo
> on Saturday, February 10th, at 10:00 a.m."

Simple, straightforward and gets the message across. That's the beauty of the "talking heads" technique: you can mould it very easily to achieve exactly what you want it to achieve.

You've probably noticed that I always use a final announcer in all of my ads who is different from the main character in the ad. That's to give it an extra oomph! It's a simple technique that allows you to re-state all the details that have already gone before in the body of the ad and I would highly recommend that you use it. Without it your ad runs the risk of dying at the end instead of leaving the listener with additional information that will help them remember what they heard in the first place.

So when you're writing your ad be as simple or as creative as you like, but never lose sight of the message that the ad is trying to get across. Get your business name and your message into the first couple of lines, and then repeat them as often as you can. Then have your second announcer at the end repeat them all again. Your listeners can't hear those two facts often enough. You've got to make use of every one of those 30 seconds to your best advantage. Only by writing and rewriting will you be able to achieve that properly, but the results will certainly make it all worthwhile.

How to think about TV advertising

I'm sure I don't have to tell you that TV advertising is expensive, but I will anyway. Not only is the time on the box very expensive, but the creation of your ad will also be a great deal more expensive than any other type of advertising because it takes a lot more people, time, equipment and expertise to make a video than it does an audio recording. Those are the facts and there's not a darned thing you can do about it.

However, if you do decide to do some TV advertising I would pass on the same advice as I did for the radio ads: keep in control. Don't allow yourself to be bamboozled by the miles of wires and the technological wizardry you see around you. It's your business and your money. Make sure it's being spent wisely.

There are other ways to make a commercial rather than running all over the countryside with cameras and fuzzy mikes. If you look in your Yellow Pages you will find multimedia companies who can create wonderful animation for you at surprisingly reasonable cost. These folk can marry together bits of film and video and create movement on their computers that you just can't believe. It's actually worth a visit to one of their studios just to see what they're up to in there.

It is also quite possible — although in my mind a little pointless given the medium of moving pictures — to simply have a still photo appear on the screen with a voice-over adding your message. If you feel you've just got to advertise on TV but don't have a fortune to spend on production, that's a method that deserves investigation.

So do look around and see what you can find that will save you money and still get your message into the public domain in a sensible way. I won't dwell on TV ads too much as I have come across very few small businesses that can afford to advertise using this particular medium. Plus, if you really want to go in this direction there are lots of well experienced people available who can help you every step of the way. Get in touch with them because you'll be spending big money and it's worth having the experts on your side.

TEN POINTS TO REMEMBER

1. Radio advertising is expensive. Can you clearly identify a time when your target audience will be listening to your ad?

2. Keep control. Your radio station must allow you to be involved in every step of the process of making your ad.

3. Make sure the package you buy from your station does not give them the decision when your ad will appear. Be specific about the time slots you want even if it is a bit more expensive.

4. Examine the opportunities for advertising at particular times of the day before or after particular regular slots, e.g. traffic news, weather forecasts, news, what's on, etc.

5. Use the excitement of radio and sound effects to create memorable ads.

6. Use the various techniques available to create ads that are different from one another.

7. Use testimonials from your customers in your ads. This is a very powerful way of advertising in any medium, but especially radio.

8. Beware of being your own spokesperson (few peo-
    ple will have the nerve to tell you your voice is all
    wrong unless you ask people you can trust for an
    honest opinion) or using humour.

9. Accept that you cannot make a TV commercial
    without spending money on professional help.

10. Make your sound and audio advertising as exciting
    as possible. It's fighting to be heard in a very noisy
    world.

7

How to Write a Brochure that Will Boost Your Sales

It's a tool every business should use

Why your business needs a brochure

I'm always surprised at the reaction I get from clients when I suggest we sit down and create a brochure to promote their business. Usually they say they really don't think it would help. Or, what could they possibly put into a brochure that anybody would want to read?

What indeed? After all it's just your business we're talking about. You certainly wouldn't want to let anybody know what you were up to, now would you!

But I can understand people's apprehension. There are some businesses where it is assumed that you will have a brochure. Hotels, for example, or conservatory sales people. So why not yours? If you run a restaurant surely your potential customers would be interested in a brochure that would show how the inside of your restaurant looks. Or they might like to find out a bit about your chef and the training and philosophy he or she has. Or how about if you operate a corner store? Surely a lot of your customers would be interested to read that you are expecting your stock of Easter eggs to arrive at a certain time, or that you will have a certain number of whatever this year's favourite toy is available if people want to place an early order. Might you be able to pre-sell a certain stock before you've even received it?

And the same principle applies to every business — even yours. Remember that your job is to communicate with your customers/potential customers at every opportunity if you're to build a real relationship with them. Therefore you must consider using a brochure to do so.

The problem with the idea of a "brochure" is that everybody has a pre-conceived notion of what it is. A brochure is an expensive piece of glossy paper with four-colour photos and reams of exciting copy, right? Wrong. Certainly a brochure can be all of those things, but I would encourage you to think of a brochure as an up market flier. More than a cheap photocopy, but a lot less than an expensive glossy promotional piece.

The beauty of modern day computer technology is that just about everybody can create an impressive piece of promotional material. If you have a computer but don't have DTP (desktop publishing) software, I would encourage you to get your hands on a cheap piece of software as soon as possible. Even the most basic computer can turn out a pretty good brochure with a couple of hours input from you (or your eight-year-old child!). And I can guarantee that you will get back the investment many times over if you take time to create brochures on a regular basis to promote different aspects of your business.

However, even if you don't have the technology in place yourself, your local copy shop will have and will be able to knock-up a brochure in a day if they're any good at all. And it won't cost a fortune.

So, now that we've dispelled the myth that brochures have to be expensive and can only be produced by big organisations, you need to know how to create a brochure that will be effective for your business whether you're using it as the main promotional tool or as a regular addition to your marketing arsenal.

How to write a brochure that works

A brochure is very different from either a print or electronic ad. There is no sense of urgency with a brochure. You have the time and space to make your offer and explain it properly. Within reasonable limits, you aren't confined by either time or space. For example, if you take an A4 piece of paper and fold it into thirds, you'll see exactly how much space you have. You've now created what's called a "gatefold" brochure and it will have 6 "panels" in which you can outline your offer. Alternatively you could fold the same piece of paper in two, or even cut it in half (A5) and fold that in half. There are as many alternatives with paper sizes as you can imagine, but if you stick with the basic A4 or A5 format you'll keep your printing costs to a minimum.

So, now look at your folded piece of paper again and begin to imagine the exciting things you could do with it. You could write a big headline on the front panel which would draw people inside and then let your message flow across the full inside, or divide it up into individual panels. You could simply have a picture on the outside and let that draw them in. Or how about filling the inside with information and using the outside panel to write addresses on and posting the whole thing?

The most important thing to *not* do is to fill every possible inch of space with photos, graphics or words. If you're looking at a white piece of paper, then determine to keep a lot of that clean white paper untouched. Believe it or not, the more "white space" you have the better. There is nothing to turn people off more than looking at line after line of tightly printed propaganda. Your customers aren't going to spend hours wading through this brochure. At best they'll read it quickly and then file the information to the back of their minds for later reference. So make it easy for them to read and get your message. Keep the pictures and words to a minimum. In fact, as a guide, decide not to have more than 250 words on your 6 panel brochure and you'll be about right.

How to write the front page

The front page is panel 1: the first panel they'll see when they pick your brochure up off your counter or pull it out of the envelope (we'll assume you're not going to use this as a "self-mailer". But if you do, then the front panel will have only the name and address and maybe a short one line teaser to get them inside).

This is your main advert. It's the eye-catcher to get them interested and it must read like an ad. In fact, many of my clients will use a headline from a recent ad to give their brochures a bit of impact and help reinforce the ad next time their customer sees it in their local rag. So, be sparse with words, make the print big and get their attention. How about:

Open
Me
and
Save
Money!

Nothing too subtle about that. But I'll bet it would work. In fact, I know it would because a client of mine who owns a small grocery store uses it all the time and can't keep up with the demand for his money-saving brochures.

Every week he produces a new brochure which is really just a list of special offers for the week along with one or two relevant pictures. He leaves his brochure round to the local copy shop on Saturday afternoon and picks up 500 copies on Monday morning. Every week he chooses a different colour than the last to make sure people recognise it as the most current copy, and by Thursday he's out of brochures. Cost to him is two hours on an ancient Amstrad PCW and printing. Benefit to him is a loyal clientele who will ignore the big supermarket at the edge of town until they know what Alan has on offer. Simple. Cheap. Cost-effective.

So we're really not talking about a need for very sophisticated brochures, here. However, we are talking about very effective brochures.

How to create the inside of your brochure

Having written your "teaser" for the front page, you need to give some serious thought to the inside panels.

Here's where you'll make your pitch. Here's where you must use your creative talents to their best advantage.

There are numerous ways in which you could lay out your inside panels. You could line pictures up along the bottom and fill in with copy. You could have copy only. You could have a mixture of pictures and copy. It really doesn't matter and all depends on how you feel you could best show what you have to offer. But a word of warning. Unless you are going to write a letter to your customers by running the copy from top to bottom of the page length-wise, do not let your copy flow over the side of the panel. Treat each panel as if it were a column in a newspaper and keep your words inside each fold. You don't have to put a new subject into each panel, but do keep them as separate columns.

We have already discussed the use of "fonts" or "typefaces" in another chapter, but it's worth repeating here that you should use different typefaces sparingly. It is important to make your brochure as easily read as possible and therefore you need to use bigger and bolder text now and again. You might even want to underline the odd piece and certain headings might be in a different typeface, but don't be tempted to use too many as this will make your brochure look both messy and incredibly unreadable. Result: it ain't read!

How to make your brochure look professional

So let's get a few "do's" and "dont's" for your brochure into print. In the end, what you put in your brochure and how you put it there is entirely up to you. But by learning a few of the trade "tricks" you will have a better chance of creating something that is worthwhile rather than something that looks like three drunk men on a committee decided to throw-up together (I use the term advisedly):

- Do be sure that your front panel is attractive enough for your customers to want to know what delights await them inside.

- Don't allow yourself to fill every inch of space available with words and pictures.

- Do be sure you know what you're trying to communicate before you even begin. If you don't know, chances are your customers won't take time to figure it out for you.

  ◊ Are you simply trying to tell people about your service?

  ◊ Are you offering them something that is based on savings of money? Or time? Or are you making yourself available when nobody else is?

  ◊ Are you selling a service? Or an innovation? Or convenience? Or a combination of a number of these?

  ◊ Whatever it is, be sure your customer will know by the time they reach the end of your brochure.

- Don't try to be too clever for your own good. The job of your brochure is to get a clear message out to your customers. Too often people are tempted to try to be clever at the expense of clarity. Don't let that happen to you.

- Do be careful with your use of words. Words like "value", "quality" and "unbeatable" are so overused as to make them meaningless. Actually, they're fairly meaningless anyway unless you can quantify them. And please do not use phrases like "we have the experience to do the job you want". I know how easy it is to say. I even understand that you would believe it to be true. But if you're a plumber and the job I want is to re-roof my house, then you can't do it! So how about replacing it with "we have the experience to be able to guarantee our work". Now there's a feature of your business that is a real benefit to me. Words are powerful. Please use them properly.

- Don't use jargon. Most of us have our noses stuck in our business so far it is very difficult to write about it without assuming that everybody uses the same jargon as we do. They don't. So write to them in a language everybody will understand. If you make your customers feel pretty silly when they're reading your brochure, you can assume they won't call to ask you to explain what you mean. Instead they'll read somebody else's brochure that explains everything simply and in a way they can understand, and then they'll call them.

How to set out your brochure

Layout of your brochure is a rather specialised job if you want more than a fairly simple black and white result. You might want to include a few colour photos or a graphic or two to add interest and depth to your message and that is exactly what the expanse of your brochure can allow you to do. However, to do it properly you will need to be able to scan your information onto your page and set it in a way that is appealing to the eye.

There comes a time when "DIY marketing" comes up against a brick wall and can go no further without the help of somebody who has a certain amount of expertise in their field and I think this is a job for a professional. As such, I always encourage my clients to get in touch with somebody who has an eye for design to help them put together a brochure that is going to work. It's worth the investment to get it right at the beginning rather than have to throw hundreds of brochures away in the future when you realise that they aren't working.

Your choice of professional is entirely up to you. I would start at your local copy shop and see if they have the facilities for bringing all the ideas you have together into a package. If not, then they should be able to put you in touch with a designer. In the days of desktop publishing, designers are easily available and you will probably find that there is a freelance or two in your area. Approach them with your ideas and what you are hoping to achieve. Negotiate an arrangement where you will pay them for any work they do that you actually use and let them put something together for you.

In the negotiation agree a fee up-front rather than agreeing to an hourly rate. That is about the most bogus way of doing business I can think of and amounts to a blank cheque. If they're any good they'll be able to give you a price and unless you change your specifications they will be able to hold to that price.

How to get your brochure printed

There are a number of ways to get your brochure printed, depending on the type of brochure you have. It is possible to simply run it off the photocopier but the word "amateur" would be written all over it in very large letters.

The minimum I would suggest is that you go to your local print shop and ask them to set the whole thing up and run you off a certain number. They will probably do it on a computer so the more you can provide them already done the cheaper it is going to be. So if you are working with a computer, ask them how they would like you to save your files so that they can read them onto their screen and work with what you have done yourself.

Modern technology can make even the printing of only 200–300 full-colour brochures a cost-effective exercise for both you and your printer, so do develop a good relationship with them and put their knowledge to work for you. The last thing you want is a warehouse full of brochures that will take you two lifetimes to distribute. Find out what your printer can do for you by asking the questions you need answered.

TEN POINTS TO REMEMBER

1. A brochure can be a real window into your business.

2. A brochure is not necessarily a glossy four-colour masterpiece. It can be simple and cheap to produce.

3. A simple brochure can be created on a desk top computer. If you have the computer, consider pur-

chasing the software to allow your to do some basic desktop publishing.

4. There is no sense of urgency with your brochure. You have the time and space to explain your offer in depth.

5. Your brochure should retain a feeling of space by leaving a lot of unused white-space. Avoid making your brochure look cluttered.

6. Work to an A4 or A5 format. It will keep your printing costs lower.

7. Make the front panel of your ad your headline. Give them a reason to read the rest.

8. Keep your copy jargon-free and easy to read and understand.

9. Use a professional designer if you feel you need one. For anything other than a very simple brochure you probably will need to buy in some expertise. It will be money well spent if their creative eye can help you develop a more dynamic piece of advertising.

10. Get to know your printer and ask all the questions you can. Use their knowledge to save you money.

8

HOW TO GET FREE MEDIA COVERAGE (1)

Getting started

Why it's important to get media coverage

No matter what business you're in, you don't need to be told that we live in a very competitive age. Every year universities and colleges churn out more lawyers, doctors, engineers and dentists than the country can absorb. And every year some bright spark decides to open a restaurant, barbershop, corner store or a mobile phone dealership right next to yours.

So no matter what profession or business you're in, you know there's going to be competition. And because there is so much competition, it's no longer enough to simply advertise your business more than the other guy. Nor is it enough to hope that because you've been around longer that your customers are going to show unswerving loyalty to you. That isn't going to happen. And not only do you have to accept that, you also have to be prepared to get out into the marketplace and into people's homes and lives as much as possible.

We've already talked about how that's done by various types of advertising, now we're going to look at the opportunities for free media coverage that are available to every business in every town in the country!

About three years ago my wife and I decided to move house. We didn't know any solicitors who could carry out the conveyancing for us so we started to trawl through the lists of local solicitors' offices to find one we thought could do the job and asked our friends, and got a few ideas there.

But when it came to the actual selection, I called the guy who did a short column in our local newspaper every week on various aspects of everyday law. He did the job well, didn't charge a fortune and answered all of our questions politely and fully.

Every single one of the solicitors in our area could have done the same job. On checking we even found that the price was around the same. But the man who had the column in the newspaper, the man who had all the free advertising and might even have been given a few pounds from the paper for his trouble, got the job. And the only reason he got it was because in a profession that is overcrowded he took time to find a way to get his head above the rest.

Now it's for you to take that example and apply it to your business. You must find some way to get your head above the rest of your competitors by taking the time and effort to claim your share of free media coverage.

Why it's important to invest time in seeking free media coverage

It will take time for you to get into the papers or onto the radio/TV. Every week press releases, telephone calls and articles land on editors' desks by the basketful — very often the wastepaper basketful — and even though yours is a busy schedule, you must learn how to develop a relationship with the media in your area that is mutually advantageous. In other words, it's not enough to simply write to the editor and say, "I've got the world's greatest sale on this week, could you please give me a free mention in your paper". His response will be to have the advertising manager get on the phone and sell you an 11 cm x 3 cm column ad!

But write and tell him you're having a local personality come and get shaved bald at your barbershop and the photographer and reporter will be there in a flash.

What's the difference? In the first instance you're asking the editor to give you something with nothing in return. In the second you're giving the editor a great "fun" picture for his front page and you are getting a bit of coverage as well. Mutually satisfying and beneficial.

There is a bit more to the whole process than that, but in the end your job is to create a story that your editor will want to cover while getting some good coverage for your business.

We've already discussed the importance of every business to work to get their head above the crowd. If you're selling something unique or offering a service that nobody else is providing, then you do not need to think too hard about achieving this because there isn't a crowd around. But when you're in a field where really there's little difference between you and your competitors, then you need to use your promotional skills to have your business perceived as different by customers and potential customers. And as those perceptions are often reached by choosing the most familiar name then it is obvious that you need good and regular media coverage.

There is nothing wrong with self-promotion. In fact, as a business you owe it to yourself and those you employ to present your business as best you can and get as much media exposure as possible whenever it is to your benefit. It is simply not enough to have a good product or service to offer. Your image and positioning in the minds of your customers is often the most important difference between success and failure. In fact, the reality is that even those who might not offer the best product or service experience the most success because they work hard at successfully communicating their message in the media.

Your task is to be the one who does the most work. Don't allow yourself to believe that there is some magic formula or ability that you either have or don't have. By following the steps laid out in this chapter you will have the tools to promote yourself properly. There might be a little art in self-promotion, but mostly it comes down to hard graft and effort. So if you're prepared to make the effort to create a story that is attractive to the media, then you'll be surprised at how much help the "professionals" (journalists, photographers, etc.) in the creative side give you in return.

As consumers we all increasingly measure the importance of a product, service or person by the amount of media exposure they receive. For example, you might have the best version of a gizmo available on the market, but if your competitor is better at getting media coverage, then the chances are that people's perception is that their gizmo will be better than yours. The media really is very powerful and you have every right to work to use it to your advantage.

And the best news about going for free media coverage is that the size of your wallet is relatively unimportant. Journalists are always looking for stories, comments and ideas. If you provide them by telephone or press release then in time you will become their "expert" in the field and will be asked for comment or background information regularly.

Your first step is to use a telephone or stamp to get your story to the right person and then help them make it happen. If your story is strong enough the journalists will do your work for you and it won't cost you a fortune to get column centimetres. And if the journalists adopt you as their "expert" in a given field then their readers will also begin to do the same. The only things you have to do is work to develop the idea, story or comment in the first place. That takes time, effort and an amount of determination, but it's worth every minute of time invested in achieving your goal of positive and regular media exposure.

Why free media exposure is more powerful than advertising

No matter what we might think about journalists and the press in general, we always make the assumption that something reported has an element of newsworthiness to it. Therefore, if something is reported we assume that it is true, important and worth taking note of.

Let's suppose you place an ad and get 10 responses. The following week a journalist writes a short piece on your product or service and you get 50 responses. Was your ad a failure?

Probably not. But the fact is that instead of simply taking your ad and believing every word of what is after all raw propaganda, your customers have taken the third party endorsement of the journalist and given it a lot more credibility. Which is the same theory we all use when we ask a tradesman or professional for references. Sure, we believe that what you say you can do is true, but you're going to add a lot of credibility to your claims if we can find others who are happy to endorse them.

The big difference between free editorial and advertising is that you give over control of the tone and content of the piece when you put it in the hands of a journalist. Therefore, you have to put thought into your initial preparations and how you might react to questions that will arise from your submission. So before you approach a journalist you owe it to yourself to approach the story from every angle you can think of, both positive and negative, and come up with the answers that might otherwise come out of the blue and leave you babbling like an idiot!

Why you need to invest time in getting to know your media

Even though we call this "free media" it's not quite accurate. You will have to invest time and energy to get to know journalists and what your local papers and radio stations want from you. And if you're looking for free coverage you have to give the reporters reasons to cover your story which will take time and effort on your part.

So the media is no different to anything else in business; you'll get out of it exactly what you put in. If you don't take time to find out what your reporters want then don't be surprised when they don't carry your story. But take time to chat with them and ask them how you can make their job easier by presenting your material in a way that they can use, and you'll be amazed how much help and coverage you will get in return.

If ever there was a "you scratch my back and I'll scratch yours" situation in business, this is it.

Why it's important to target your message

If it is your job to create your own news, it is also your job to make it interesting to your target media. For example, if you're a butcher you would be wasting your time sending a press release to a vegetarian magazine no matter how well presented your message might be.

Slightly less obvious perhaps, but even more important, it is imperative that you take your story and write it in various different ways highlighting certain features that will appeal to different segments of the media. Do not simply come up with a brilliant idea, write a generic press release and then send it out to every newspaper, radio station and magazine you can think of. Think everything through first.

For example, a client of mine is a new car dealer. He sells executive-type cars and is always looking for new ways to get a story into his local newspaper. So when he realised he had sold his 1,000th car he decided to get some serious coverage and gave me a call.

First we looked at the local papers and decided to go with a simple "car dealer sells 1000th car" story with the proud owner and his family being photographed with his new car. Naturally we gave him a bottle of champagne and bunch of flowers and tied a big bow over the bonnet to make the photo more attractive. We also had a local racing car star present the keys.

Then we put together a story about the growth in executive car sales regionally for our local paper. It talked about how people were trading up in their choice of car and used the 1,000th customer as an example with a few quotes from him on why he had chosen this car.

Next we got our racing car star onto the local radio station news talking about careful driving and how bigger cars were safer to drive.

Then we got an article into the classic cars magazine based on the idea of today's cars being the classics of tomorrow.

Finally, we got a small picture and 150 words in the regional business magazine where we had the new owner — a prominent businessman — talking about how he felt it was important to enjoy the fruits of your labour.

One story and five different interpretations which hit home and guaranteed my client a lot of coverage because they were "packaged" in a way that was attractive to the target media. There may well have been more opportunities available if we had taken time to think it through further, but other restrictions and demands took precedence.

And this is exactly how you should look at the opportunities that your business offers you to do the same thing. No matter what you're doing, there are people who want to read about it. And more importantly, there are journalists who want to write about it if you "package" it with an angle that makes sense to their publication or station.

Why the media want to hear from you

So you own a small business in a big city. All around you there are big businesses and corporations who hog the limelight and take away every opportunity for you to get a look in, right? Wrong!

Turn on your local news this evening, or look in your local, regional, or even national newspapers and make a note of the stories. Sure there will be the big boys stealing the front page headlines, or getting mentioned at the top of the hour, but what comes next? Invariably there will be a story, or even a number of stories, that centre around smaller organisations, businesses or even individuals. Why? Because journalists know that as well as reading all about the lives of the rich and the famous, people love to read stories about other people who are just like them. They want to hear about the business that came up with a great idea and boosted sales. Or the one that decided to dress all the staff in false faces at Halloween. Or the one that thought it would be a good idea to start a collection of cans of food to be sent off to a third world country in crisis.

Use this desire to your advantage and start getting your stories into the papers and onto the news. You might not see a rise in takings the next day, but over time people will begin to identify your business with success. And people love success. They love to read and hear about it, they love to identify with it and most importantly they love doing business with it.

5 ways to give your story the hook it needs to succeed

Every story needs a "hook" — something that will make it interesting and a little different. Something that will catch the attention of a journalist and make them want to know more.

So you've got to find something that makes your story newsworthy and not simply an advert for your business. Look in your local paper and you'll see stories that are repeated on a regular basis: boy wins competition; circus comes to town; local flower festival proclaims winners. They're perennial stories, but they are newsworthy and therefore get printed. Your job is to create the hook that will make your story newsworthy, and there are a number of tricks that work every time.

1. Everybody loves a good fight

Not very positive perhaps, but everybody loves to read about the small guy taking on the big one, the David versus Goliath scenario. A good disagreement, division or court appearance is grounds for a story.

2. The "est" technique

This is an easy technique for making your fairly mundane story take flight by adding something that makes it exciting. The "biggest", "fastest", "longest", "shortest" will always get some coverage.

So if your opening the biggest store, selling the longest sausages or bringing in the fastest service, then get the story out. And if you don't have anything that qualifies as an "est", then create something.

A butcher that I know — but unfortunately don't do any work for! — decided to sell the "longest sausages in town". Each sausage was going to be 24 inches long and sold at the same price as regular ones. Now that might not seem terribly interesting, but he got a picture and 250 words in the local rag because of it and I'll bet he enjoyed a brisk trade for a few weeks as a result.

So try and get some "est" into your life!

3. The "th" technique

We all love to read about people who have made it to their 100th birthday. And we also love to read about businesses that have served the "th" hamburger, reached their "th" anniversary or provided their service to their "th" number of customers. The "th" technique is strong and makes a great headline for your local paper. Become aware of anniversaries or events that get an "th" into your story and you've got a press release that just about writes itself.

4. Make it local

National and regional news is important, but everybody loves and reads about local stories.

So your story has to be a local one if it's to be of interest to local papers. Chances are your business is a smaller localised one, but if you have a number of outlets around the country, make your story apply to your local store/office. That way you can be sure of getting the story into every relevant local paper rather than being hidden on page 30 of the regional one. But when you're approaching your regional or even national paper, radio station or TV station, then make sure you present your story in a way that will appeal to them.

5. Add a benefit

There are two words that catch everybody's attention: "how to". Show people how to do something and they'll love you forever.

For example, a restaurateur client of mine decided he wanted to get some fairly constant coverage for his business without having to pay for it. Looking around for a "hook", he realised he had it already in his chef who was known throughout the area for his fantastic desserts. In fact, he always held the suspicion that people would scoff down their main courses to get to the dessert trolley as quickly as possible!

So we decided to use the chef to promote the restaurant. Noel, the owner, approached his local paper and offered to have his chef give away a "secret" recipe every week if the paper would give him a column. No problem! And so now Noel and his chef sit down every week with a recipe and create a short column which tells people "how to" make the dessert of the week.

Have people stopped coming to the restaurant? Not at all. In fact even more people come now to see how the finished article should look before returning home to present it to their friends at their next dinner party.

It's a winner because they've shared a secret "how to" and helped people become better at something they love to do: eat and impress friends.

TEN POINTS TO REMEMBER

1. We live in a competitive age in which every business has a responsibility to raise its profile above the heads of its competitors.

2. There are acres of free column centimetres waiting for stories about small business successes in every local, regional and national newspaper in the country.

3. Self-promotion is not a bad thing and if your business happens to benefit from a good story being printed in the newspaper or told over the airwaves then that is because you have offered something that is of mutual benefit.

4. Consumers measure the importance of a product, service or business by the amount of media exposure they receive. Your task is to promote your business and so take advantage of that credibility in the minds of your customers and potential customers.

5. To benefit from free media coverage you need to take time to research the needs of your local print and electronic media.

6. By "packaging" your story in different ways to appeal to different audiences you can achieve a high level of coverage.

7. Your story needs a "hook" to make it interesting. The "est" (biggest, longest, fastest) and "th" (anniversaries) techniques often work the best.

8. Local papers want local stories. Always make your stories relevant to the locality.

9. Don't be concerned that by sharing your knowledge with people you will lose customers. People might want to know "how to" do something, but they'll still come to the professional to get it done.

10. Every business in every sector in every town in every country can get as much free publicity as they can handle if they take time to find out what their local media want, and then give it to them!

9

HOW TO GET FREE MEDIA COVERAGE (2)

How to write a successful press release

I love writing press releases because I know that if it is a good one I will see just about every word I've written in print in my target paper or magazine. I guess I'm just a frustrated journalist at heart!

But the beauty of a press release is that it is the one piece of promotional literature that pretty much writes itself. With a bit of attention to format, you will be able to write press releases that will present your business and your story in a way that will definitely get the attention it deserves and more than likely get picked up and used in one way or another. By following a few simple rules your press release will stand out from the reams of paper that cross a journalist's or editor's desk and will catch their eye as it moves swiftly from fax machine or envelope toward the wastepaper basket.

Who, what, where, when and why

When you're writing a press release you are providing some very specific information to a journalist. What you are not doing is writing a short novel. Therefore, you have to have it follow a particular route to communicate the information in a way he or she will be able to pick up on quickly and will leave them looking for more. Just enough to give them the information they need to whet their appetites, but not so much that they won't want to pick up the telephone and get more details from you.

And that information needs to be communicated in a format that is accepted in the industry: the "who, what, where, when and why" format. By writing your press release in a format that answers these five questions you will create something that a journalist can identify with and which will lead them through your story in a structured way.

Who?

The "who" of your press release should appear in the very first sentence and will refer to a person, group or business. Sometimes the very "who" can be the most interesting piece of the story and will make the journalist sit up and take notice from the very beginning. If you've got a movie star coming to open your new store don't hide the fact way down in paragraph five. Get it right up front.

But even if your "who" is an as yet unknown organisation or business, it is the place to start to let the journalist get a handle on exactly "who" they are dealing with from the start.

What?

What is this story about? Obviously this needs to get up into the first paragraph or two to give some meaning to the story. So do not confuse this part of your press release by listing a number of points you would like the journalist to cover. Select one important point and get it done in simple language. You will have all the time in the world to develop other sub-themes in your supporting material.

Where?

Where did or will this story take place? Location is of great importance to journalists who will want to put the story in context. If you're writing to a local paper and talking about an event that happened in a city 50 miles away, your chances of getting any coverage are slim. But relate that event in some way to their locality and they will want to know more.

In the example I've given, the millionth hamburger might have been served at a location miles away from the outlet in town (b), but if the story is made relevant to this store then it will get coverage.

When?

When did, or will, this story occur? Obviously journalists are very aware of deadlines and they will want to have some specifics on this story regarding times. If you're promoting an event that will happen in the future then schedule it with these deadlines in mind and your story will get much better coverage than if you simply schedule it for your own benefit.

Why?

Why is this story so important that a journalist should give up valuable time and space to cover it? Everything before this was a preliminary to the importance of the story and you need to be sure that your "why" is very strong unless — as in our example — you've created a "fun" story that is probably going to end up as a photograph and 50 word piece to support it.

Any Business	Contact: Bob Jones
Any Street	Tel: (01222) 333222
Any Town	Fax: (01222) 323232
	email: theman@dot.com

For Immediate Release

<u>Any Business Sells Its Millionth Hamburger</u>

Any Business sold their millionth hamburger from its shop in Main Street, Anytown today. Congratulating the millionth customer, Mr John Spokes (36) Bob Jones (Chairman of Any Business) said that this confirmed his belief that hamburgers continued to prove as popular as ever.

Smiling as he enjoyed his millionth hamburger with his family, Mr Spokes told reporters that he visited Any Business regularly with his family and looked forward to eating the two millionth one as well!

Staff of Any Business presented Mr Stokes with a bottle of champagne to enjoy with his millionth hamburger, but he decided to keep it for another occasion explaining that he was driving home and wanted to make it a safe journey.

Any Business was started in Another Town in 1973 and has grown to a chain of 35 restaurants positioned in high streets throughout the country. The restaurant in Any Town was opened in 1981 and employs 35 full and part-time staff. Every new member of staff is fully trained no matter what position they hold in the company.

Mr Bob Jones, founder of Any Business, explained that the company had been built as a family business serving families. "All of our staff appreciate the importance of families being able to eat out together. So even though we might be a fast food chain, we always take time to appreciate our customers and spend a little time getting to know them. We like to think of ourselves as an extension of the family kitchen. An opportunity for mum to take a break from cooking by offering good nutritious food at prices that are real value for money."

-end-

Along with this press release I would also enclose a picture of the happy Mr Spokes and his family enjoying the millionth hamburger, some additional information on the company, a picture of Mr Jones for reference and a copy of the company training policy if there was a short one. Then the journalist would not only have the information on the story of the millionth hamburger but also an idea for a story on staff training or the operation of chain stores in the town. Mr Jones would have the opportunity to call in a few days and see if there was any further information he could forward that might help in the formulation of a story which he might even suggest at that time.

Almost as important as the story itself is the format your press release is written in, so let's take a look at the format of this press release, which has really written itself based around the story of the family with the millionth hamburger.

How to give your press release a professional look

If your press release is to be taken seriously it needs to follow certain rules which make it stand out from the rest of the crowd. Apart from the actual content of the press release itself, you will need to pay attention to a few additional points that will help make your journalists life easier and therefore raise the possibility of your story making it to print.

1. Who is the contact?

After the journalist has decided they are interested in your story they need to know who to contact for further information. Some PR people put the contact name and numbers at the bottom of their releases, but I think it should go right at the top. After all, this is a story that is important, right? So the journalist should know at first glance who it's from. Plus when they are looking for a telephone, fax or e-mail number they don't want to have to take time to try to find it. If it's right there at the top they can get whatever information they need quickly and efficiently.

The most important thing is to make sure the contact name is the right one for this story. It has to be the person who knows the most about the details and can be available to answer the questions. You should also double-check that the telephone and fax numbers are the correct ones because you can be sure the journalist isn't going to waste valuable time looking you up in the telephone book.

2. When can the story be used?

Most releases can be used immediately and the line "For Immediate Release" will let the journalist know that is the case. Sometimes, however, you might want to get the information out to a journalist before the event has actually taken place.

This is more common with political releases than in business, but let's say you are having a grand opening of a new shop on Monday, 1 October. You get your press release out to the media the week before to be sure to get coverage on the day, and to prevent any paper announcing your Grand Opening before the day itself you would put an "embargo" on the news, that is, a note that the information is not to be used before a date and time which you specify.

In practice it would read "Embargoed until 8:00 a.m. Monday, 1 October." Chances are you won't ever use that technique but you should be aware of its availability and use it if you need to.

3. Give them a headline

Even though I'm in the word business, I often have difficulty coming up with catchy headlines. However, I think it is important to give the journalist an idea of what your story is about right up front rather than simply launching into the story with no announcement of what it's about. Chances are some clever person at the paper will come up with a catchier headline than the one you think of, but the idea at this stage is to get the journalist's attention and then let them worry about how they're going to caption the story itself.

4. Give them a little bit extra

In our example we have Mr Jones talking about his commitment to families in his restaurants which he feels is the reason his company has grown so big. This has little to do with the actual story, but it does give the journalist a nice quote if they want to talk a little about the ethos of the business. So there is a place for a bit of extra relatively unconnected information in your press release.

5. Make it double-spaced

For a journalist to work with your release he or she will want to add notes and information in the relevant parts. Therefore, it is necessary to leave them enough room around the edges and between the lines to do that. Double-space your lines and leave wide margins for notes.

6. One page should do it

You're not writing an epic here, simply giving them the facts. So try to make your press release no more than a page long. It's not a sin to be longer, but it might suggest a lack of discipline on your part. No story should need more than a page to get the basic message over. After all, you want to leave your journalist looking for more information and having to call you for it. So don't overwhelm them with every minute piece of detail at this stage.

7. Make it hang together

It is possible that your story will not be earth-shatteringly important, but will be interesting enough to be given a few moments on a news bulletin or centimetres in a newspaper.

If that's the case a journalist will be have the task of rewriting your press release into a particular format without actually calling you for more information and taking the story any further than you've presented it.

That's why you need to make your press release hang together in a way that the journalist can use. In fact, you want to give them a press release that they can use almost verbatim.

The trick here is to make each paragraph self-sufficient, i.e. not depending on the one before or after to give it context. Look at the example again. Read any paragraph and you will find that it is a story on its own and does not require any more information to support it. Each paragraph gives new information but could be lifted and quoted on its own and still make perfect sense.

If you do this you make the journalist's job much easier and so raise your chances of having your press release used. They will change things around a little and add bits to bring the story together, but you will have provided them with the bones of the story which they can simply lift straight from the page and use.

8. Support your statements

There are a couple of reasons to send support material along with a your press release. The first obvious one is that it adds credibility to your statements and puts them in context. The more important your statement or claim, the more important it is to support it with articles from other papers or magazines, graphs or even a video tape if you think that will do the trick.

But equally important is the fact that the more information you send a reporter the more ideas you're going to generate in his or her mind. For example, a reporter might decide to profile your business if your supporting material looks interesting enough. Or he might see an aspect of your business that would support another feature in the paper that they have been working on. If nothing else, you can be sure that you will become recognised as a potential source of information for future pieces and that can prove to be very important and influential.

With all of the supporting material we would send with our example you can bet Mr Jones would be approached for a comment on BSE when he would have the opportunity to assure customers about the quality of the beef in his burgers, or even plug his response to the problem by introducing the new chicken burger.

If there is a feature on business in the area Mr Jones will be called for a comment on the general economic situation. And if the local council decide to re-rate businesses, Mr Jones will pop up again with a comment or two.

In short, by providing a complete history, support and story, Mr Jones' number is going to find its way into the journalist's list of contacts and in due course he will have the opportunity to either be quoted directly or direct the piece by being a source of back-up information.

And that's how your business can benefit too if you make the decision that this is an area worth investigating and investing in.

How to avoid the pitfalls every novice falls into

The last thing you want is for the journalists you are approaching to recognise you for the novice you are from the very first line of your press release. There are a number of mistakes that everybody can make without even thinking about it, so try to avoid them as best you can.

1. Avoid jargon

Your journalist will have been around for awhile and will probably be aware of your business and what you're up to. But no matter how much he or she knows about your business, they will not try and wade through a press release that starts,

> Mr Smith is proud to announce his fly turning gizmo at 3/4 speed will connect with a ramrodding supercharger to create a fantastic new widget end at 30 degrees to the perpendicular.

Go that route and you've lost before you've begun. If necessary, test your press release by giving it to someone who doesn't know much about your business. If their eyes gradually glaze over while they read, it's time to start again!

2. Keep it honest

It's incredibly easy to be over effusive in self-praise with a press release. After all, you probably do believe yours is an "earth-shattering" discovery or "the most miraculous breakthrough in the history of baking".

But it's not, and you have to accept that journalists won't believe outlandish statements or claims. Indeed, not only will they not believe them this time, you'll have to work twice as hard next time to even get them to acknowledge what you have to say. So try and kerb your enthusiasm and remember to write to your jaundiced audience. Keep it honest and fairly low key. If the journalist decides it's a "world first" then they will be sure to put it in their copy. But let them decide based on the facts which you give them.

3. Presentation. Presentation. Presentation.

Try to remember that a press release is not just another piece of paper. This piece of paper contains claims and support for a story which will hopefully bring you more business. That makes it very important and means that you must assume that the person who will be reading it has never been into or even passed your business. They have no idea who you are or what you do.

With that in mind, your press release becomes your "shop window" to them. If it's dog-eared, poorly written and full of spelling and grammatical mistakes, it says a lot about you and your business. But if it's presented on pristine white paper with maybe a short cover letter, some well organised pieces of support material and carefully constructed and proof read, then that says you're for real and should be taken seriously.

You want the journalist receiving your press release to take you seriously, so do them the same courtesy please. It will be worth the time and effort, believe me.

Check your press release

Does your press release pass the "Walker Five Point Test"?

1. Does it present your main point in the first sentence?

2. Does it have all the salient information in no more than one page?

3. Does it hang together and is every paragraph self-sustaining and complete?

4. Is it free of all grammatical and spelling errors?

5. Does it have all the necessary back-up and support material attached?

If the answer to all five questions is yes, then get it in the post immediately. If not, then you've got a bit of work to do, but at least you're on the right track.

How to make your press release personal

We've already talked about "packaging" your press release to particular journalists by emphasising different points in your headline and first sentence. But there is another equally time-consuming but possibly more profitable way of doing it.

If we assume that journalists are as human as the rest of us (which they are), and they love to get a bit of personal recognition (which they do), then it would be fair to assume that a personal letter to a particular re-porter might be read before a mass-mailed press re-lease. And even if we choose to send a fairly standard press release but have a personal letter which points out how we think their readers might benefit from the information accompanying it, then not only will we be able to develop a personal contact between the jour-nalist and ourselves but we can take a second opportu-nity to promote a particular angle on the story.

As with anything worthwhile this will take time, ef-fort and a commitment to research, finding names of particular reporters to whom to write. But the divi-dends will make the investment worthwhile. After all, the whole point of this exercise is to get media coverage so if it takes a few more minutes to create personal let-ters but they result in better coverage, then I say do it! And if a hand written note works better than a com-puter generated letter, then work on your handwriting.

TEN POINTS TO REMEMBER

1. Your press release is being sent to professional journalists and therefore must conform to their protocols. There are particular rules you must ad-here to in the layout of your press release which will help determine its success.

2. Your press release must answer the "Big Five" questions: Who; What; Where; When and Why. These questions must be answered in this order and must be answered in a way that makes your story exciting enough to command the journalist's attention.

3. You must provide journalists with the names of the right contacts and the right telephone and fax numbers where they can be reached for more information.

4. It is possible to send a press release prior to the time that you want the news released. However, you must remember to place the embargo information prominently near the top of the press release.

5. Your press release must hang together in a way that makes each paragraph self-sufficient and able to be lifted from the page without losing its context.

6. You must be prepared to support the claims you make in your press release by providing the necessary back-up information that will give your claims substance and depth.

7. Your press release should be as jargon-free as possible.

8. You have a responsibility to yourself to provide only 100 per cent honest statements of fact. Your credibility will be damaged irreparably by trying to palm-off half truths or grossly inflated claims.

9. Your press release must pass the "Walker Five Point Test" before you send it.

10. If you take time to "package" your press releases to specific journalists rather than sending a generic release to them all, you will get substantially more free media coverage.

10

HOW TO GET FREE MEDIA COVERAGE (3)

How to turn your message into news

How to work with journalists

So now you've decided to get a slice of the free media that is available to every business in every city, town or village in every country of the world.

You've sat down and taken a good look at the opportunities your business has for getting some coverage, and you've got a few ideas of how to give it some "spin" to make it attractive to a journalist. It's got a hook or two, maybe an "est" or an "th", and you're ready to take the plunge. How do you approach your local media and get your story into print or onto the airwaves?

First, let's look at a few journalistic realities. Reporters have a responsibility to their reading/listening public to provide real news. They do walk the streets looking for leads, ideas and stories, and they do have certain amounts if newsprint to fill and deadlines to meet. As such they are always open to hearing about a good solid story.

However, they do not have a responsibility to promote your business or use any half-baked story that lands on their desk. And just because you ply them with home-made goodies or free product doesn't mean they have to present you and your business in a good light. In fact any reporter worth their salt will refuse to accept gifts if they think you're giving them with thoughts of favours in return. So you do need to approach your local journalist with a solid story in mind rather than try to buy them off with some ridiculous stunt.

When you approach a newspaper or radio station with an ad in one hand and a cheque in the other you'll be listened to and taken seriously immediately. But when you approach the same people with a story idea, you've got to make it interesting and honest enough to get picked up. And the more interesting the better.

If you've got something that will make page one then you're king of the castle. But if your story is good but not earth shattering, then you might have to work a bit harder to get it covered properly. And a lot of that work actually takes place before you even approach the journalist by creating a press release they will want to read and follow up with.

5 rules for approaching a journalist

1. Get the right one
Don't try and pitch your story about shaving your head for charity to the political reporter. Find out which reporter covers particular aspects of the news and then get to them personally.

2. Don't waffle

Reporters are busy people just like you and they've always got one eye on the clock which moves very fast when a deadline is nearing. So, don't waste their time. Give them the bones of your story in two or three sentences, and then ask them if they want to know more. If they do, great. If they don't, say thanks and leave it at that. Your credibility will not be damaged because your story is not used. But you simply won't be taken seriously ever again if you insist that your story is important when the reporter has made it clear that they're not interested.

3. Don't try to be an editor

If a reporter decides to cover your story you will have every opportunity to give them all the details you think are relevant. Then you have to stand back and let them do their job. You cannot insist on seeing an article before it's printed or try to guide the reporter on the way they choose to cover your story. Be prepared for them to try to find somebody who is going to give a different point of view than yours. As long as you are sure that you've covered every angle before you make the initial call you can be confident that the story will reflect favourably on you.

4. Don't be a fading violet

Just because something you've done or said reflects well on you and your business does not make it bad for you to turn it into a story. There is something in most of us that says it's wrong to get involved in self-promotion, but if you have a story that is interesting enough to print and just happens to reflect well on you then you have a responsibility to get it into print or onto the airwaves.

5. There's no such thing as an "exclusive"

If you have ever advertised in the media you'll know that as soon as you raise your head above the parapet you are considered fair game by every advertising manager in the area. One ad in a local paper will result in calls from every other advertising department in every other media outlet telling you why you should be advertising with them either instead of or as well as the one you chose.

Likewise, when you get your story into one paper you're going to hear from all the others and your local radio station as well. Depending on the level of interest your story raises you might find your name — and that of your business — plastered all over the media for a couple of days. Your customers are going to think you're very important, and your competitors are going to wonder how you managed it. Brilliant!

You might also find that others approach you as a result of your coverage. A local organisation might ask you to be a spokesperson because they liked what you had to say, or how you said it. Or you might even be approached by a political party to consider standing for local government. So be prepared to hear from all kinds of interesting people as a result of your efforts.

You might not take up any of the requests or suggestions, but your life is going to be a lot more interesting while you listen to them talking!

8 ways to win a journalist's respect

No matter what business you are in there are a number of protocols that will enable you to do certain things and restrict you in others. These are recognised ways of doing business that have developed over time and allow everybody to conduct their business in a way that is considered "proper".

Journalists are the same. They have developed systems that allow them to get to the heart of a story without appearing to be biased or obliged to any source of material and by being aware of the imperatives of this system you can win the respect of your reporters and prevent yourself from making a mistake that might damage your credibility in the future.

1. Get your story right

That is, word your story in a way that is going to make sense to your target journalist. We've already looked at the example of how we got a lot of coverage for our car dealer by "packaging" different aspects and slants on one story geared to the needs and interests of particular markets.

Unfortunately, this is very time-consuming, but it's worth doing if you want to milk as much coverage from a particular story as possible. Sending one generic press release to every media outlet is hit and miss at best, and a complete failure at worst. You wouldn't dream of writing an ad or brochure that covers every possible market for your business, so don't do it with your promotional work either.

2. Try to give your story as much "muscle" as possible

If you are making a claim about your service or business, then back it up with as much relevant information as possible. For example, if you are sending a press release about a campaign you've started to gather clothes to send to refugees in a crisis area, back it up with information about the charity you are affiliated with, some information on the region the clothes are going to and even a graph showing how the situation has deteriorated over the past three years. By adding this to your story you're not only giving it more credibility, but you're also giving the journalist a lot more material to work with. So instead of a small picture and a few words on your efforts on page 20 you might find yourself part of a major review of the situation along with your efforts on page 5. And if you can provide photographs, no matter what story you're presenting, you'll add real weight to your story.

3. Respect your own, and your journalist's, credibility

No matter how they might be perceived, the great majority of journalists are honest, hard working men and women. They are not interested in half-truths and questionable sources and they will stick with a story until they get the truth. So you should respect both their credibility and your own at all times, and only deal with absolute truths.

Frankly, you are the one who has most to lose if you try to sell a half-truth. Not only will your misleading information be shown up for what it is, but you'll never have an opportunity to get positive press again. On the other hand, you will find your name in lights for every small mistake you might make in the future.

If your story is strong enough and warrants coverage you will find yourself well treated and well thought of if you are up-front at all times.

4. Journalists have deadlines too

We all work to the clock. Your business will have opening and closing hours and you need to have certain deliveries by certain times if it is to function properly.

So do journalists. In fact they live and die by deadlines. So there is no point in presenting a journalist with a story at 2:00 p.m. on Wednesday if their deadline is 1:30 p.m. And it is absolutely counter-productive to expect a journalist to take time to talk with you at 2:55 p.m. if they have a news bulletin to prepare for 3:00 p.m.

Make a few calls beforehand and do some research on all of the media you want to approach, making notes on when their individual deadlines are. Then present your stories at times when they will be able to listen to you and pay attention to what you are saying. This is a courtesy that will be greatly appreciated and will show your journalists that you are as interested in them as you would like them to be in you.

5. Be available

Just because you have presented a journalist with a story does not mean that it will always work to your advantage. There are times — rare though they thankfully are — when a journalist will take what you've said and contact somebody who will try to refute it entirely. This won't happen when you are simply trying to get a promotional piece printed, but if you have taken any sort of controversial stand you can bet there will somebody on the other side who will question your comments.

In that event, your journalist will come back to you with their comments and ask you to respond. Do not shy away at this stage. If you do you will lose credibility, leave the field open to the other side and suffer a PR disaster rather than a success. Be available to answer questions and answer them fairly and honestly. If you do not have an answer promise to find one and then get back to the journalist. If you have thought the whole thing through carefully in advance you will be aware of any potential problem areas. But if you are confronted with something you haven't thought about, keep your cool and find an answer. If you give a full and honest answer you will probably find that it is enough to overcome the objection and the piece will get back on track again.

6. *"But you're my friend . . ."*

Just like you, journalists are business people. Their business is to print the news and they cannot allow personal relationships to get in the way of that at any time. That's not to say you should immediately ignore everybody in the media business, but do not expect friendship to give your story any extra weight or create a blind eye to a mistake or two on your part.

7. Put your brain in gear before you open your mouth

In the heat of the moment we can all say things that we really don't mean. We can run down a competitor or question a business practice very easily. But trying to build yourself up by putting other people down is not a good way to do business and should be left to the politicians. Be careful what you say when you are being interviewed and always be aware of how an editor's red pen can change the tone of a written piece to be very different to what you actually meant in person. Stay positive and upbeat and allow the facts to speak for themselves.

8. Don't expect anything

Don't expect your story to be printed just because you've gone to the trouble of writing it. Don't expect your photograph to appear in the paper just because you've gone to the expense of having a professional take a beautiful 8"x10" glossy. Don't expect a reporter to report your every word and don't expect your story to be printed this week just because you respected a journalist's deadline and have given them every opportunity to cover your story in time.

When you're looking for free media exposure you put yourself at the mercy of the journalist, their editor and other breaking stories. By being helpful and presenting stories that are interesting in good time for a deadline you can greatly raise the odds in favour of your story being covered. But nothing is guaranteed and if you fail this time, just get back to the typewriter and try again. And again. And again. In time your efforts will pay off.

How not to be your own worst enemy

There is no question that journalists are always looking for stories to cover. It's their lifeblood and if something is well presented and relevant they will usually give it a whirl and follow it up. However, it is very possible that having gone to the trouble of developing a story idea and presenting it perfectly, you will still manage to trip yourself up and bring your own story to a rather abrupt and unceremonious end. Here are a number of ways to avoid such a result:

1. Don't fly blind

Be prepared to personally give a journalist all the assistance they need and do not allow unqualified or unknowledgable staff to handle reporters' questions. After a couple of strange answers to questions any reporter will get tired of listening to babble and hang up.

2. Do be available

We've already talked about being available to answer uncomfortable questions, but you also need to be available to answer any other questions a reporter might have. If you're not available, have your staff/secretary give the reporter a specific time when you will be — and then be!

3. Do be as good as your word

If you tell a reporter that you will give him or her some information which will remain exclusive until a particular date, then do so. Once it's been covered by that reporter you can talk to all comers, but keep your word and keep your credibility.

4. Do justify your statements

If you say you've got the longest sausages in the world then be prepared to prove it with backup material. You must be prepared to back up your statements and not simply expect journalists to take your word for it because you've got an "honest" face.

So it is entirely possible for you to promote your own business and get the free media coverage that is sitting waiting for every business in the country if they would only get off their behinds and go looking for it.

You do not need any qualifications to be your own promoter and you now have everything you need to go out and get the information that will allow you to present your story to its best advantage.

As such, you probably do not need the services of any public relations consultants that can be found in the yellow pages. It would be difficult for any small business to justify employing one of these consultancies as they probably wouldn't have enough work to make it worthwhile and they definitely would not be able to justify the expense.

That's not to say there is no place for PR professionals. There are many large companies fighting for the last 1 per cent of market share who need the best PR firm around to do it. But the vast majority of small businesses do not need a professional and can get brilliant results by going it alone. And if your story is really good and you present it as best you can you will get the coverage. That I can guarantee.

You might even have the same experience as the owner of a small convenience store in southern England who developed a "loyalty bonus programme" in response to the building of a large supermarket at the edge of his town. Little did he expect to find himself the subject of attention by national papers, radio and TV when he sent a short note about the programme to his local paper. But the idea was interesting and novel enough to get a lot of attention.

Do you have anything that could do that? I bet you do — or could have if you thought about it. The secret is not to keep it a secret. To get the information about your business out to as many people as you possibly can and get it out for free!

With some practice and a lot of research you will surprise yourself at your own success. So start now and see just how quickly you can get coverage in your local press and on your local radio station.

How to best use your communication equipment

Every office and business in the land is now blessed with an array of newfangled ways to communicate electronically with people all over the world. The telephone, fax machine and computer with modem means that everybody can reach anybody at anytime, night or day.

Unfortunately, the number of people who have learned the various protocols that go along with these pieces of equipment are few and far between. As a result every journalist in the land is overwhelmed with phone messages, fax and e-mails — most of which are either left unanswered or get scant coverage.

If you approach your journalists carefully and thoughtfully you will reflect a respect which they will recognise and respond to eagerly. By using your electronic communication sparingly you will build credibility that is all important to anybody hoping to get good media coverage.

My own personal rule is that unless a piece of information is particularly time-sensitive — and frankly, very few of them are — I prefer to use the regular postal service to get my press releases out: snail-mail as opposed to e-mail. And my thinking goes like this.

Like you and me, journalists are very busy people. Every time they have to take a phone call they are interrupting something they're already working on. (Journalists will always take a call because they just don't know when the next front page story is coming in and they won't take the chance of missing it). So if I interrupt a journalist who is working on a piece for tonight's paper or evening news with information that isn't absolutely relevant to the moment, then I know I just won't have their full attention on the telephone.

On the other hand, I am loathe to send a piece of mail that I haven't already discussed slightly with my journalist friends. So to deal with the dilemma I always make a phone call before sending my piece and word my call the same way:

> "Hello, Joe. It's Gavin Walker. Do you have two minutes for me now, or would you rather I called back when it's more convenient?" (They invariably say "Go ahead" because by now they know that if I say two minutes I mean two minutes.) "OK. A client of mine is announcing a new range of products next Thursday at a press conference at the Town Hall. Can I send you a press release and some back up information?"

That's it. No long list of what the products are or a menu of the goodies I'll have there to make the journalists feel well fed and loved. Just a quick phone call to "flag-up" what I've already got in an envelope with his name on it! Very seldom does a journalist say no to receiving information on anything — after all, information is what they live on.

So, now I've made a personal contact and the journalist is going to be looking out for my information in the post. If I've interrupted them at an important moment of the story they're working on, it's been brief, to the point and effective. On the other hand, if they have a bit of time on their hands they might ask for more information over the phone and that's a bonus. But usually they simply want to get back to what they're doing having acknowledged their initial interest.

Notice also that at no time have I asked them to commit to covering my story because no journalist will ever agree to cover any story until they have every last detail, and asking them to do so is both amateurish and ineffective.

By the time you pick up the telephone you should know that you have a story worth covering. That being the case, there is no need to pressurise the journalist. Let the facts be the strength of your story and let them speak for themselves.

How to use the telephone to your best advantage

So, your initial contact with your journalists by telephone should be brief and to the point. A quick hello and goodbye will do the trick. But there are a number of other areas of etiquette that are necessary to watch if you want to be taken seriously by the media and here they are.

1. *Always return their calls*

Boy, do journalists hate it when people ignore their calls. First you've taken time to get some information to them, and then you ignore them when they respond to your advances and call you back. You don't have to stop everything to take a journalist's call, but you should get back to them as quickly as possible.

2. *Overcome your fear of answering machines*

I hate it when I go to check my messages and get one quiet moment after another and journalists hate it even more. Whether you end up talking to their answering machines or somebody else in the office, do leave a message. And make it a full one. A journalist would rather have a message with a string of numbers where you can be reached at different times than have nothing. Leave full messages of who you are, why you're calling, and at least one phone number.

3. *Respect their time*

We've already talked about being brief on the initial call, but that also extends to every other call you might place. Yours is not the only story a journalist will be working on so appreciate that and give them the details they need to be getting on with it. If they decide they want to take time to find out all about your family history, that's great. But don't offer unnecessary information.

4. Don't be a pest

Once you've made your initial contact and have followed it up with your press release, don't pester your journalist with unnecessary calls. When a conversation begins with "I'm just calling to see if you received my press release", journalists switch-off. This is not going to be a productive call at all. They have your information and they'll get back to you when they have the time and the need to do so.

5. Let them bypass the voice mail system

A recent reaction to the preponderance of phone calls for many businesses has been the introduction of a voice-mail system. For those that have it, a secretary often acts as a barrier to calls. This is very annoying for a journalist who needs to get a response from you and you would do well to provide direct telephone numbers when possible.

A few facts about the fax

It used to be that people would raise their eyebrows if you were trying to do business without a telephone. Nowadays the same reaction is kept for those who don't have a fax machine. Interestingly enough, the fax machine was actually invented before the telephone, but that's a subject for an other book!

When the fax machine was a rarity, people were impressed to receive one. Nowadays many businesses — and newspapers in particular — could paper their walls many times over with the amount of fax paper that is wasted receiving unsolicited and useless faxes.

With that in mind, you should be sure to use your fax machine sparingly when communicating with the media. If you want to be taken seriously — and you do — then you should never send an unsolicited fax unless you are transmitting some earth-shattering news about the imminent fall of government or a local nuclear holocaust.

Not only will they be a menace to the receiver, but unless they are specifically addressed to a particular journalist, they won't make it past the first wastepaper basket.

If your journalist requests a fax, send it. If you have alerted a journalist that you are sending a fax and he or she has agreed, send it. Otherwise, use the postal service. And if you are sending sensitive material remember that a fax machine usually sits in the middle of the office and is seen by every journalist, cleaner and message boy around.

In short, only use the fax machine when you are absolutely sure it is the only sensible thing to do and there are no alternatives.

When to use e-mail

I know it's contrary to public opinion to say so, but I haven't figured out why e-mails are so popular. They take the same time as a letter to prepare, they aren't particularly less expensive than a fax and most packages don't allow you to lay them out in a striking format. So what's the big deal?

Certainly if you are communicating with people in Timbuktu or the depths of the Amazon jungle they make a lot of sense. But if you're sending a message to somebody on the other side of town I can't see the benefit. It's up to you, and if you have invested a few pounds in the latest computer just to have access to e-mail then I'm sure you'll have loads of reasons to disagree with me, but that's just how I feel. So my suggestion would be to avoid e-mails unless it's the arrangement you've made with the journalist for communicating your information.

By the way, if you do disagree, please call me, or send me a fax or letter. It's been three days since I checked my e-mails and I'm quite confident there aren't too many waiting for my urgent attention. But then, maybe I'm just not that important!

How to become the local "expert" in your field

You've probably noticed that very time you turn on the radio or television there are the same few people spouting off about one thing or another. The cookery programmes all seem to have the same faces as do the gardening ones. So how did these people — or your local equivalent — get to be the recognised experts in their field?

Well the answer is simple. First they made sure they had a good knowledge of their subject, then they came up with a gimmick or idea. Next they made themselves available to the media. Then the media took them and made them the "experts". In short, none of the "expert" chefs, gardeners, solicitors, farmers or other representatives know much more than the average person in their field. They simply know how to promote themselves.

And now that you do too, you can become the "expert" in your chosen area in your field of knowledge. By making yourself known to your local media outlets and being available to answer questions and give a bit of background information on various things, you will become well known to journalists and will be called upon as their "expert". Then the day will come when you are asked to appear on a radio or TV programme to share your knowledge and that's when your behind-the-scenes work with the journalists will begin to pay-off. Now you will really cash-in on the free media coverage.

When that call comes you need to be ready and prepared to say yes at a moment's notice. Whether it's to be a member of a panel discussion or a one-to-one interview, you will have to take time to prepare yourself for the ordeal.

The easiest way is to have a member of your family or friends act as an unfriendly interviewer or member of the audience. Their job is simply to try to ask you annoying and embarrassing questions and generally to try to trip you up. You should encourage them to be as unfriendly and unpleasant as possible and really try to get you worked up. In the meantime, you have to take them seriously and accept that whatever they throw at you could also be thrown at you by a member of your audience or an interviewer who has just had an argument with their spouse before getting you in front of the microphone or camera.

Now the chances of this happening are slim. Unless you've decided to run for public office or are trying to convince the public to give you vast sums of money with no obvious return you will find most interviewers and audiences to be fairly pleasant and co-operative. But that's not to say that they won't come up with some off-the-wall questions to which they will expect an answer. So you need to have the warm-up session first to be ready to answer anything that's thrown at you.

Once you have the first interview under your belt you will become a lot more confident. And that confidence will build as your experience of being interviewed grows. But never allow yourself to become complacent as you will simply be setting yourself up for a rather unpleasant fall on the day that the awkward questions begin.

When an interviewer asks you a question the last thing they want is a "yes" or "no" answer. They expect and want you to elaborate on your answer even if it appears to you that what you're saying is common sense and known by everybody. It's not. And the interviewer will want you to get your answers into a format that informs without rambling on forever. That is a very difficult thing to do, especially if you're talking about something with which you are intimately involved. You need to be able to get the message across in plain easily understood sentences that hang together to make a good answer to the questions. You need to practice it until you have it right.

By taking time to be "interview friendly" and being able to answer the questions that are put to you, you will very quickly become recognised as the local "expert" in your chosen field. And the beauty of this is that once you have made a good impression with your local media you will find yourself called upon again and again to make comment or get involved with an article that is being prepared. You will also be taken a lot more seriously if and when you might get involved in some other aspect of life that needs media coverage.

How to get on radio and TV

To a lot of people the very idea of appearing on radio or TV is frightening. But if you've decided it's something you want to do because you want to become the local "expert" in a given field then what's keeping you?

Well, we've already talked about working with the newspapers and waiting for the call to come from the electronic media to appear, but there is a rather quicker way to do it. A rather more direct way. Write and tell them you're around, you're qualified to talk on subjects A, B and C, and you're available!

Now that sounds far too pushy for many of us reserved people, doesn't it? But the reality is that you could sit for a lifetime waiting for the telephone to ring with the big opportunity. So if you are genuinely interested in promoting your business by becoming the local "expert" then here's what to do.

First, call the stations you are targeting and find out who produces particular shows that you think you might have something to contribute to. A business call-in on radio perhaps. Then put together a press release about you and your business giving as much detail as you can about who you are and what you can talk about knowledgeably. And then send it to the station (along with a photo if you're approaching a TV station).

While you're at it, why not put a few programme ideas into your cover letter? Suggest a programme on how local business copes with computerisation perhaps. Or if you are a plumber, how about a phone-in programme about preventing problems in the winter months? It might not be enough for a 30 minute programme, but it would certainly make for an interesting 10 or 15 minutes and it would give you the opportunity to show what you can do for the station.

Once your information has arrived you can expect a call from the producer, or maybe even from the host. They'll talk with you for a few minutes and see how you answer a few basic questions. Do you waffle, or are you succinct? Do you use jargon or can you present your case in a language everybody will understand?

If they feel you're interesting enough and can carry a conversation, then there is an excellent chance that you will be asked to appear on one of their programmes in the very near future.

How to prepare for that first media appearance
Now I know from presenting my own radio programme for a number of years that most people expect the radio station to be a very plush affair altogether. More surprise then when you turn up to find yourself ushered into a small booth where you'll share a table with the host and any other guests that might be appearing at the same time. Take notes with you if you can. You'll have the space to lay them out and as long as you don't rustle your papers you'll be able to refer to them as often as you like.

If you're taking part in a phone-in programme be prepared for a few off-the-wall questions. Otherwise you shouldn't have too much trouble. Remember that you're the expert and will probably know more than the callers on your chosen subject. But keep your answers simple enough to understand and to the point. The host will want to get as many questions from the listeners as he can.

And remember that there are more radio stations than the ones in your local town. If you have some good reason to do it, you can write to producers in stations further away and suggest you do a telephone interview "down the line". Stations don't love doing it, but if what you have to say is interesting enough and there's no way you can get there in person, they'll certainly use you.

TV is a whole different game. Not only will you have to spend a bit more time on your choice of wardrobe, you'll also have to be able to present your topic in an interesting way that will set you above a lot of others. It's a tough medium to break into, but the good news is that it is always on the look out for new "talent" or ideas. If yours is good enough and you "present" well, you have a good chance of getting the opportunity to make an appearance.

Both of these electronic media bestow a certain importance on the people who appear on them. Even though it seems like everybody and their mother has appeared on TV or radio at some time or another, your having done so will give you and your business a real lift. You will have added credibility and your customers or potential customers will recognise you long after the appearance itself. And if you are able to, become a regular media guest so your credibility and tag of "expert" will grow.

And if you really want to go for it in a big way, write to your local radio station and suggest you actually either present a programme or contribute something to a particular programme on a regular basis. If you really think you can carry it off, insist on a meeting with the Programme Director and send a tape of your voice.

That's what I did so I know it works. And if it worked for me you can be sure it will work for you. All it takes is the confidence to carry it off and the gumption to make the initial contact. Try it, you'll love it!

How to plan, promote and present a brilliant press conference

A press conference is a very dodgy thing. It might allow you to reach a lot of media representatives quickly, but you've got to have something very important to say before they'll turn up to listen to you. In short, there might never be a time when you have to take the step of calling a press conference, but if you do, here's how to do it — brilliantly!

How to plan your press conference

As with everything to do with the media your planning will have to be exact. But what makes a press conference different to a press release is that you have to facilitate the needs of the hordes of media men and women who will expect to throng your given location.

Location. So, first things first. You've decided your subject, bombshell, news release does demand the status of a press conference and will be interesting/ important enough to command the interest/attendance of the press. Before you even send out your invitations to your press conference you have to decide where to hold it and the location you choose needs to meet a number of criteria:

- Is it easily found? No point in having it in some warehouse deep in the middle of an industrial estate. Even if that's where you do business, move your press conference to a location that's easy to find.

- Is it convenient? Do not expect journalists to travel miles to your press conference and then fight to get a parking space. Make it as central to the various media you will be inviting as you can. A local hotel with a decent car park is a good standard.

- Is the room accessible? Once at your location you don't want reporters wandering hallways trying to find you. Make your room as easy to find as your location.

- Is the room adequate? Make sure your room will be comfortably warm and well lit. You'll need a number of seats, a table or lectern to make your presentation from, and a bland backdrop behind you. You'll also need a sound system to be sure of being heard and enough space for TV cameras if relevant.

Timing. Remember that journalists have a deadline to meet. Unfortunately they all have different deadlines depending on their schedules, therefore I would recommend you time your press conference for mid-morning around 10:00 a.m./10:30 a.m. Most journalists will find this good for them, and if the content of your conference is sufficiently important (which it will be or else you wouldn't be holding it), then they will have time to get a piece filed for the important midday news.

In the same vein you should be quite positive that your press conference will run for a particular length of time, and stick to it. Half an hour to 45 minutes will normally be long enough for a presentation and questions and answers. Get that timing into your press release and your journalists will know you're not intending to keep them forever.

On the other hand, if you're having a press conference in the new restaurant you've featured in your press release then you might invite them to take lunch with you. Whatever you decide, make sure you put it in the release to let them know what they're committing to before they even leave their office.

Your guest list. If you're at the stage of needing a press conference you probably have a full list of all the relevant journalists in your area. But take time to review that list and add or take away names as appropriate. A press conference is also a good opportunity to make an impression with people who might not actually be members of the media but are equally important to your operation. For example, if a local councillor has been particularly helpful in guiding through planning permission you might like to "reward" him or her by inviting them along to your conference and getting them quoted. Needless to say, you should be 100 per cent positive that what they have to say will be relevant, positive and absolutely non-controversial.

How to promote your press conference

Your first goal is to get as many different journalists to the press conference as you possibly can. You've got a great announcement to make, you've chosen a great location, and now you have to write the press release of your life to build the interest into a commitment to attend. You'll need:

- A press release
- Press information packet
- Invitation.

Creating a press release that is good enough and exciting enough to get a journalist to attend a press conference is almost an art. Don't kid yourself into believing this is going to be anything other than difficult.

Then you also have to create the packet of information that will give the story real meaning and depth. Attached to all of this should be an actual invitation to attend the press conference with all the pertinent information — time, location, etc. — clearly written in.

Get it to your target journalists in good time, and then follow up to get a commitment from them to attend. This is one of the very few times when it's acceptable to start a conversation with "I'm just calling to check that you got my information"!

But when you call be sure to give the journalist some good solid reasons to attend — reasons not to simply lift the story from the information they already have. A demonstration, perhaps. Or the opportunity to meet an important person connected with your project but who isn't usually available for interviews.

How to present your press conference

Now it's time for you to pull out all the stops and let your creative mind get to work. Your press conference needs to include a lot of information, opportunities for photographs and interviews, and as much theatre as you can include that won't take away from the main event.

For example, a client of mine was quite determined to have the local press experience the new state-of-the-art video conferencing suite they had installed in his hotel. It was an absolutely incredible piece of equipment and it introduced video-conferencing into the area for the first time.

Because his was a hotel it wasn't too hard to find, had plenty of car parking space and a great reputation for its finger-buffet which was well advertised in the invitation.

When the reporters arrived, however, they found the seating arrangement different to the usual "theatre style" seating arrangements of press conferences. Instead of sitting in rows facing a podium, they found themselves sitting around a long conference table which had one end pushed hard up against the wall.

At the appointed time, the hotel owner entered the room, welcomed the reporters and told them that he had absolutely nothing to say. Instead, they would have the opportunity to directly question the developers of the equipment. With that he pushed a few buttons, the lights dimmed, the wall at the end of the table slid open quietly to reveal a screen and almost immediately the pictures of the developers appeared — sitting at a table that looked like an extension of the one the journalists were sitting at. The effect was very dramatic as it appeared that the journalists were sitting around the same table as these guys and talking directly to them — in Japan!

Now that was pretty impressive and a very nice piece of theatre. You might not be able to stage something quite like that, but get creative about your press conference and make it a little different to the usual. Journalists sit through some pretty dreary monologues from people that think what they have to say is more important than the journalists' time. But show a bit of respect for the journalists, give them something a little different and not only will they stay awake throughout your press conference, they will be more eager to see what you might come up with at any subsequent ones!

You should also take time to fully prepare yourself and any speakers you might have at your press conference. You've gathered the local media to this impressive event so don't expect them to leave without asking some questions. That's their job and even if you've plied them with cold lobster salad and Chardonnay they'll still want to ask questions and won't feel obliged to make those questions particularly easy if something strikes them as important.

Stage a mock press conference beforehand if you can, especially if what you're announcing is in any way controversial. Get all the questions out on the table and practice the answers thoroughly before you go into the spotlight. Believe me, there is nothing worse than finding yourself stumbling over an answer to a question you had not expected. A mock press conference beforehand is time well spent.

Even if things aren't controversial, make sure you have answers for everything including how your gizmo works, the technical specifications and the type of material used to make it. Get well briefed and give good solid answers.

If you follow these guidelines you will probably have a great press conference and will get all kinds of positive coverage in all the media in the area you cover. You'll have put together a very professional package that will build your credibility with the press and add to your profile in the broader world.

There are a lot of reasons why you should have a press conference (give the journalists hands-on experience, a chance to speak to somebody who doesn't have the time to do the media round, an opportunity to ask specific questions about a particularly complicated subject), but there are as many reasons why you should not and I would encourage you to think carefully before committing yourself to a press conference as opposed to taking time to do individual interviews. Such an event can save you a lot of time and energy, but let's look at a few reasons why you should ask yourself . . .

. . . Should I have a press conference at all?

There are a number of reasons why a press conference can turn from a potential promotional coup to absolute disaster and you need to be aware of these difficulties before you begin.

Just because you've invited them doesn't mean they'll be there. Journalists have a lot of call on their time. Your press conference may not be the only one scheduled for 10:00 a.m. on Tuesday morning, and unless you actually have something of more importance to say than the other fella, your journalists will go there for fear of missing a better story.

Journalists are competitors too. Journalists don't really relish being treated as a mass of people. They have egos which enjoy believing that they are the best reporters and are working for the best paper/news station in the area. Therefore, they have a certain reluctance to attend a press conference where they'll be getting the same information as the cub reporter on the free newsheet down the road. So that's why you've got to have a real tangible reason for them to come along.

And because they're competitors they're going to try to prove they know more than the other guys by asking questions. And their question will be topped by another until, if you're not careful, the whole thing can get out of hand. The last thing you need is to have a TV camera trained on some egotist who is asking you questions you'd much rather not answer at this particular time, or on which you might be a bit weak.

Bringing together different media means you lose the opportunity to "package" your story. We've talked about how important it is to present your story with different slants to different media and expanding on their particular interest. But with a press conference all of that goes out the window and you present the same information to the whole herd and hope they each take what you want them to take from it. In short, you relinquish a certain amount of control over events when you substitute a press conference for an individualised press release.

Don't despair. There are many reasons for having your press conference and for making it an absolutely fabulous affair. But please think carefully before deciding to hold one in favour of the one-to-one interview or press release.

TEN POINTS TO REMEMBER

1. Treat the journalists you are approaching with the same respect you would give any other professional person.

2. You have the task of winning the journalists' respect by showing that you have taken time to learn about their business before approaching them personally.

3. The most important part of a journalist's life is their deadline. Use your knowledge of their individual deadlines to present your story at the right time and prevent being rejected because of bad timing.

4. Be absolutely 100 per cent sure of your facts before you commit them to paper for presentation to any journalist.

5. Use modern communication equipment sparingly. Unless your news is particularly time-sensitive you can afford to use the regular mail rather than fax machine or e-mail. However, if you are going to use either, then alert your journalist to watch out for it first or it will get lost in a busy office.

6. Being recognised as the local "expert" in your field will give added credibility to your business. It is

worth working towards and you should be prepared to work with local journalists to achieve that goal.

7. When you are given the opportunity to give an interview either to a print journalist or on the electronic media, prepare well in advance to allow for full answers to predictable questions, and relevant answers to unusual questions.

8. Think carefully about using the technique of a press conference. But if you decide that it is the only way forward, then give yourself the time to plan, promote and present it brilliantly!

9. Schedule your press conference at a place and time that will ensure the highest turnout of all local media.

10. Be sure to make a note of which journalists were unable to attend and get follow-up information (including a transcript of the press questions if possible) to them as quickly as possible.

11

How to Use Community Relations to Build Your Business

A healthy community = a healthy business

How public relations is different to "community relations"

Public relations and community relations are very closely linked and related, but for the purposes of this book I have recognised a very important difference.

Public relations is all about self-promotion and building the image of your business through the media. In return you expect to build the profile of your business and get a measurable response that will directly affect your bottom line.

Community relations is about getting into the community and building a relationship with it without expecting any measurable return on your investment of time and/or money.

Every one of us knows the man or woman who gets involved in every high-powered committee and organisation in town with the express purpose of getting their name in the paper as a local do-gooder. Their "community relations" efforts are calculated to get them coverage and win them financial gain. That's all there is to it and it's pretty obvious.

But we all have to recognise that our business does not exist in a vacuum. Our business is a part of a community and we have a certain responsibility to get involved with the community to make sure it is secure, healthy and growing. By giving of our time and even a little money now and again we can be sure that our business will thrive because we are sure we are living in a thriving community. This is not about self-serving opportunism where you get the name of your business on the backs of the local football team. It's about enlightened self-interest where your community thrives and your business thrives because of it.

How to manage business responsibilities and community responsibilities

You are a part of your community and you and your business have a vested interest in making sure that that community is healthy and prosperous. You need to be sure that the services — schools, hospitals and emergency services — are up to scratch and financed well enough to service the community. And you need to know that the planning laws aren't so stringent as to keep new blood from moving into town. But your prime responsibility must be to your business and the people it supports. Your family and employees expect you to pay attention to their welfare and security ahead of running in an election to become a local councillor.

As a community minded business person you will have more opportunities to get involved with your community than you can handle. Learn to say "no" when necessary and don't bite off more than you can comfortably manage. If your business fails through lack of attention you won't be remembered as the man or woman who spent every available minute campaigning for the new school building. Instead you'll be remembered as the poor sod who couldn't manage their business properly. Take your interest in community relations seriously, but do keep them in perspective.

And of course there are times when you can use your community service to help your business without being particularly obvious about it. If your local Chamber of Commerce is asleep why not work with it to develop a few good ideas that will help everybody involved. Maybe a charity effort that will let you help your community and get a bit of advertising in local media as an extra incentive to you to organise it and others to get involved.

And if your business ties in nicely with a local organisation then get involved with them and don't shun any positive publicity it puts your way. For example, a hotelier client of mine was approached by a local sports team for sponsorship and he readily agreed to help. He didn't ask for anything in return for his small cash donation. In fact, he gave more than they had asked for. Now his local rugby team use a room in his hotel for all of their meetings and get-togethers. He doesn't charge them a penny for the space, but you can bet your life they don't leave his premises without gathering in the bar for a drink and he gets first refusal on all their social events. A simple example of how his completely unprofitable gesture became very profitable indeed.

By allowing local events to advertise on a board on your premises you will also be providing a very important community service. You won't make any money from doing this, but you might find the people who come into or past your premises to check the board spend a pound or two in your business. It's not terribly difficult to get involved and the potential rewards in both recognition as a business that cares for its community, and possibly even for financial gain, is great.

How to operate successfully in your business community

By business community I mean anybody with whom you might either be supplied by or supply to, as well as the greater community in your town or region. These people are important to you and need to be co-operated with — even the ones that you consider to be your competition.

Let's look at the example of a small client of mine who sells hardware. She has a very impressive array of merchandise, but guarantees that she can get anything you need in hardware within 48 hours. So there are a lot of people who use her shop from surrounding towns and villages even though they have small hardware shops nearer at hand. And they use her because she delivers on her time promise.

And how does she do it? Very simply: she maintains a very close relationship with all of her suppliers. She knows the birthdays of the reps and their family members and makes sure she doesn't miss an opportunity to speak to any of them when it presents itself. Result: all of her suppliers think she's the best thing since sliced bread and will turn cartwheels to try to help her when she calls with a request for a particular item. She has a very specific plan for business relations in place and it works.

You need to treat your community business people with the same sort of approach. They might not be able to benefit you directly and some of them might even be in direct competition with you and your business, but it is to your advantage to work with them. You might want to consider joining a local traders' group to get to know some of them better. It mightn't bring you any particular immediate financial advantages, but any time you need to work together for the benefit of your town, you'll have a few first names to call upon. Or how about when your local councillors decide to do something daft? A few calls to people who will at least recognise your name and be able to put a face to it will put you way ahead getting things organised.

People like to do business with people they know and your business community relations strategy will help you get into that position.

How to react to the political community

Most business people are too busy to actually get involved in politics and the few who do are probably very well established and a little older. As a result it is very easy to ignore the political community both locally and on a regional basis. But you shouldn't. Your community is governed in many ways by the whims of the politicians. One stroke of their pen can affect the viability of your town or even the street in which you do business.

What happens in politics should therefore be of interest to every business person. Not that you should spend free time at Town Hall listening to endless meetings. But do be aware of what's going on and make a point of at least getting on first name terms with your councillors. Because, when the time comes for you to get politically active, it will help your business immensely to know who to call.

But you're thinking to yourself that you will never need to get politically active. And maybe you're right. But what about the time when the council decides to paint double yellow lines right in front of your business? Or what about the year that your rates go through the roof because of some overspending on the part of the council? That's when you will have to get active. And that's when you will be ahead if you've taken time to develop a loose "political community" strategy.

How to get your employees on your side

There is little point in working hard to get a great strategy in place for promoting community relations in your business if your employees aren't working with you. And as with everything else in people management, your first job is to involve them in the programme.

Let your employees know that you are a business which cares about the community and everything that entails. You care about the welfare of your customers both inside and outside your business. Without telling them that's the case — and asking them to help you make your strategy work by making suggestions and passing on names of potential contacts — your employees might not work against you, but nor will they be working with you.

You need to set high standards in community relations for your staff to follow. You need to be prepared to let them go to community functions even if it means they're away from their desk for a few hours. They need to understand that they represent your business even when they're off duty. You need to encourage them to get involved in community projects and support them when they need it.

By involving your staff — even if you only employ one person for a few hours every Saturday afternoon — you can reach further into the community than you could if you tried to do it all by yourself. And your staff will respond very favourably if they have the pride in knowing that they are working with a company that cares for more than just the bottom line. That you care about the community of which you and your staff are members and are prepared to invest a little time and money to help make it function a little better.

TEN POINTS TO REMEMBER

1. Public relations is about developing your profile. Community relations is about developing your community.

2. Community relations is a not-for-profit activity that might result in great amounts of profit.

3. The success of your business takes priority over any community relations project. If your business fails you've failed your community.

4. Your community relations efforts might well result in direct positive publicity and that's OK.

5. You need to set high standards for yourself and your business in your community.

6. Your business does not operate in a vacuum. The overall health of your community is important to the overall health of your business.

7. Even something simple like allowing local organisations to advertise on your premises shows that you're a caring member of the community.

8. You should treat your "business community" with an attitude of co-operation. Your business community includes your suppliers and your neighbours. It even includes your direct competitors!

9. Political community relations are important even if you have no political affiliation. Local politics impacts on your business and you should take every opportunity to acquaint councillors and other politicians with the impact their decisions have on the business life of your community.

10. Community relations can impact directly on your employees. Let them know what you're up to. Let them know you're prepared to support them in their own efforts at community relations and they will feel an allegiance to your business. By showing them that you are interested in the community in which they live they will respond with a loyalty and desire to help.

Appendix

DICTIONARY OF ADVERTISING AND PROMOTION TERMS

Acorn

An industry method of classifying people by the neighbourhoods in which they live.

Advertising

The art of successfully communicating what you have to sell to a target audience by way of paid-for promotion.

Air time

The amount of time you buy from radio and TV stations to advertise in.

Artwork

A final layout of the both copy and illustrations ready for printing. This term can apply to both laser printed sheets from a desktop publishing package to a full layout by professional designers.

Advertorial

Publication or programme (radio and TV) where the editorial content is influenced, controlled or even produced by the advertisers.

Background

Information usually accompanying a press release which is used to add depth to a story and confirm certain claims made in the press release.

Budget

Your advertising budget can be determined by either taking a set percentage of gross sales, basing your spend on past figures, or determining the required level of spending on advertising according to the "buying cycle" demands of your particular business.

Business to Business

Advertising done specifically from your business to another. The details and theories of the advertising are the same as for consumer ads, but the content might be different.

Business Reply

You can provide would-be customers with a business reply envelope or card by applying to your local post office for a licence. There is an annual fee and you are charged per piece of mail handled during the year. you can provide either first or second class postage.

Buying Cycle

The cycle your business will experience based on the needs of your consumers. This will be determined by their specific requirements at certain times of the year. For example, a domestic oil supplier will experience a cycle that rises during the winter months and falls dramatically during the summer, and there is little he can do about it. Advertising schedules should take buying cycles into account at all times.

Campaign

Advertising campaigns are carefully thought through uses of various media with specific targets, aims and goals in mind. They can be one-off campaigns that last a week, or they can be longer campaigns with various parts and steps to reach the desired result.

Cluster

A group of people or businesses grouped together by location, interests or business.

Communications

Advertising is all about communications and sometimes using the word "communicate" rather than "advertise" focuses your mind on what you are actually trying to achieve: to communicate your message to your target audience.

Community Relations

Realising that your business does not operate in a vacuum and needs to be involved with the community in which it is situated without any requirement of return

on investment or time. A healthy community will ensure a healthy business.

Consumer

Your customer.

Contacts

Your contacts are a very important part of the success
of your business. People like to do business with people
they know and your contacts will help build your business.

Copy

The technical term for the words you use in your advertising to sell your product or service.

Copywriter

The technical term for the professional in an ad agency
(or possibly freelance) who will write your copy for
you if you don't feel able to do it yourself.

Creative Director

The individual in the ad agency who co-ordinates all of
the various parts of your campaign from copy to illustrations to photographers, etc., etc.

Customer Profile

A profile of the habits and preferences of the majority
of your customers. used to determine where and when
to advertise. For example, if a high percentage of your
customers are younger, female, successful business-
women, then do not advertise in the *Sun* (working class

and male-oriented) and do advertise in *Cosmopolitan* (female-oriented, middle class and career-minded).

Database

A manual or computerised listing of customers' names, addresses, telephone numbers, product preferences — in fact any information that will help you do more business with your customer base.

Deadlines

What journalists live and die by! A particular day or time by which the journalist must have completed and filed their story. Different media have different deadline times and you would do well to find out what they are if you are planning to work with the media.

Demographics

Criteria used to group a population according to common personal or financial considerations. For example, working class, middle class, employed/unemployed, earning up to £8,000, £8,000-£15,000, etc.

Desktop Publishing

Computer software which allows personal computers to create newsletters, brochures and other printed advertising.

Direct Mail

The ultimate weapon for the small business which allows you to get specific information into the hands of a specific target audience relatively inexpensively.

Direct Response Ads

Ads that are created specifically to encourage the reader to respond immediately. Rather than simply describe the product or service it asks for the sale.

Display Ads

Ads that contain headline, illustration and text.

Editorial

A body of copy that describes and discusses a particular topic. It is usually written by a reporter or commentator and contains a certain amount of their personal response/feelings.

Electronic Media

Radio and TV are considered electronic media. Internet advertising would also qualify in this category

Embargo

A time restriction placed on a press release by the author. Usually reflects the release of information to the press prior to it's being made available to the public. An "embargo" prevents the press from printing the information.

Features

When media dedicate an amount of space to one subject it is called a "feature". There might be a feature on your town, your industry or your business. Each "feature" could be used as an opportunity to sell relevant advertising.

Features and Benefits

A powerful way to present your product or service by pointing out the features of what you have to offer, and then describing how that feature will benefit the purchaser. Selected features and benefits should vary to be relevant to the target audience.

Freepost

This is a business reply method which can be provided upon purchase of a licence from the Post Office. You will be charged per piece of mail and certain addressing requirements will need to be fulfilled.

Fourth Estate

In Europe during the middle ages there were three "estates": nobility, clergy and common people. The press didn't fit into any of those definitions and so in the early 1800s the term "Fourth Estate" was used to define them. In short, the press is separate from everybody!

Graphics

Any type of picture, cartoon, photograph, graph or matrix used to give a visual feature to support your copy.

Headline

The eye-catcher that stops your reader in their tracks and draws them into the body of your ad.

Hot Buttons

The particular features and benefits of your product that appeal to your target audience. Specific points you can use in your ads knowing that they will motivate your customers to buy. For example, charities will often use pictures of child poverty to motivate people's generosity.

Hot List

A mailing list that you know will work. Names and addresses of customers who have bought from you in the very recent past. A good "clean" list, fresh enough to avoid too many useless addresses.

Illustrations

(see graphics)

Image (photographic)

Often photographers and other ad professionals will refer to photographs as "images".

Image (business)

How you present your advertising as a reflection of your business. Using ads to create an "image" of your business in the minds of potential customers.

Interview

Opportunity to put your points-of-view to a journalist either directly over the airwaves or through a reporter who will create a story around your comments.

Insert

A printed piece about your business or a particular offer that is included with a magazine, newspaper or catalogue that is designed to generate enquiries or direct orders.

Jargon

Using words that are specific to your business. Jargon should be avoided in all consumer advertising but is permissible in business-to-business ads.

Jingles

The art of communicating your message in song! Some jingles are remembered for decades, but most die an ignoble death.

Key Code

The code you would imbed in a print ad to let you know where the respondent saw your product advertised. A means of monitoring the effectiveness of ads helping make decisions on which magazines, papers or even ads are doing the job for you.

Libel

Printed information that is untrue, defamatory or harmful. It's OK to have views and opinions of your competitors but be careful how you word your thoughts.

List Broker

A professional company which has access to a great number of mailing lists which we can rent for a fee.

These brokers should be able to create a list according to your specifications from their database.

Logo

A special design that identifies you and your business on sight. A powerful piece of advertising that encompasses all of your public image in one small graphic. Think of McDonalds' "Golden Arches" and a whole raft of perceptions follow on.

Mail Order

Goods or services sold by mail. Or goods and services sold from ads that require a direct response.

Mail Shot

The name given to each individual direct mail campaign. Posting 500 or 5,000 letters would be considered a "mail shot" if they were all the same letter with different addresses.

Marketing

"Marketing is producing and selling at a profit goods or services that satisfy a customer's demand."

Market Research

Taking time to discover what your customer and potential customers want from your business. This information can be used to drive your advertising or change your mix of stock.

Media

A collective term which describes more than one communication outlet.

Off-the-Record

A comment made to a journalist which is agreed to be non-ascribable to you. However, assume that everything you say to a journalist can and will be quoted.

On-the-Record

Opposite of off-the-record.

Packaging (press releases)

A term used to describe how you might present the same story in different ways to different papers or magazines. The slant of your story would be "packaged" to appeal to their market.

PAF

"Postal Address File": A post office compilation of all UK addresses which is available on CD-ROM.

Phone Feed

An interview with a radio station which is conducted down the telephone line as opposed to being live in the studio.

Positioning

"What a product or service does, and who it is for" is the official definition of positioning. However, it may be more easily understood as the positioning of your product or service as high as possible on the ladder of importance that is in the mind of every one of your clients.

PPO — Printed Postage Option

A printed stamp on your business return cards and envelopes that replaces the normal stamp and can be used by licence from your post office.

Press Conference

An event which is so momentous as to require the members of the media to gather together in one place to discover the details and life-changing consequences of your discovery, invention or business. To be successful it requires an important announcement and no small amount of theatre.

Press Release

Written information presented in a particular format with the intent of raising interest in the media.

Proofreading

Reviewing a written piece to ensure there are no typographical or grammatical errors.

Promotion

The art of presenting your business in an interesting and eye-catching way to media and customers alike.

Public Relations

The aim of your public relations is to create or maintain a favourable climate of opinion in which your business can operate.

Question-and-Answer Sheet

A sheet of information which accompanies your press release to add depth to the claims you make in your release asking and answering what you think might be questions journalists might think of.

Reporters

People whose job it is to find, research and report the news.

Response Rate

A method of measuring the success of a direct mail campaign based on the percentage of respondents. From a "cold" list 1 per cent would be considered a fair return, where you would want 3-5 per cent response from a "warm" or "hot" list, that is from lists that you have compiled of known customers.

SFX

A notation used in radio scripts to determine the need for "special effects".

Slogan

A phrase you might use to sum up your image. Who could forget "Guinness is good for you"?

Sound Effects

Available in all radio stations, sound effects allow you to place your ad anywhere at any time. In a car, on a train or set in the jungle, sound effects create an atmosphere that helps the listener suspend belief for 30 seconds.

Split Test

Using two or more ads to promote your goods or services and measuring the success of one against the other. The ads might be completely different or might simply make a small difference in presentation or offer, but a "split test" can sometimes help in the initial stages of an ad campaign.

Sponsorship

Where your business donates money to a particular cause, event or group of people in exchange for having your business either mentioned — perhaps in a programme — or emblazoned across the chest of a junior soccer team.

Target Audience

A specific group of people you are hoping to reach through radio or TV advertising.

Target Market

A specific group of people you want to have consider your business as their first choice.

Testimonials

Statements from your customers confirming that they have benefited greatly from the service or product you provide. A powerful third party endorsement of your business.

Time Sensitive

Being aware of journalist's deadlines and providing them with information well in advance of that time.

Typeface

A style of lettering also referred to as a "font". The choice of typeface can convey different impressions and ideas and the choice of type size can determine the legibility of the written piece.

Voice-Over

In TV the voice that is used to describe a picture is called a "voice-over". The same term can also be found in radio advertising.

INDEX